We

close

each

prayer

with

AMEN

IT'S ALREADY DONE

IT'S ALREADY DONE

IT'S ALREADY DONE

AAALACAPIRINGAUTHORS@2021

AAALAC & ASPIRING AUTHORS MAGAZINE

P.O. BOX 2031

MYTRLE BEACH SC 29578

- KINDLE: B09F2LRSMB (PUBLISHED 8/30/21)

- PAPREBACK: 9798520994435

3 WOMEN & A TABLE
CONTENT
PRAYER

I.   OPENING PRAYER pg. 9

II.   LEARN- pg. 11-133
Cheniera Osbourne

III. LOVE- pg. 135-257
Pamela J Hayes

IV. LEAD- pg. 259-383
Angela Thomas Smith

V.   CLOSING PRAYER pg. 384

DEDICATION

This book is dedicated to all of GOD's children seeking a closer walk with him. HE LOVES YOU NO MATTER WHAT!

Feb 1, 2021 Cheniera , Pamela and Angela went on a 121 day prayer sabbatical standing on

Psalm 121 I lift up my eyes to the mountains—

   where does my help come from?

2 My help comes from the Lord,

   the Maker of heaven and earth.

3 He will not let your foot slip—

   he who watches over you will not slumber;

4 indeed, he who watches over Israel

   will neither slumber nor sleep.

5 The Lord watches over you—

   the Lord is your shade at your right hand;

6 the sun will not harm you by day,

   nor the moon by night.

7 The Lord will keep you from all harm—

   he will watch over your life;

8 the Lord will watch over your coming and going

   both now and forevermore.

FOREWORD

Sh'Aunta Moore

You know, when Angela asked me to write the Forward for this phenomenal Affirmation Book, I was very humbled and a bit afraid all at the same time. You see, I don't take it lightly that God continues to choose, use, and send me as He sees fit. So, with that being said... #HereWeGrow..

One of my favorite scriptures in the bible states that we must renew ourselves in God Daily. Not when we think about it or feel like it, just simply do it every day. Cry out to Him (God) when you cannot see your way. Remind yourself that in the face of adversity, we are still his chosen people. In today's time, there are so many false prophets, and confused people, that is hard to believe what you see, and most of what you hear. Stress being the lead cause to early deaths because of the toll it takes on one's mental and physical ability. Clouding our simplest thoughts and loading our minds with doubts, and weights that we were not meant to carry. I know that I am not the only one. With all of this, HERE WE ARE! Still striving, still yearning, still hungry for the clarity and calmness of God. That makes us ALL the Just Man that the bible calls us. We know that without a shadow of a doubt that God will never leave us nor forsake us, so we continue to Fight!! We Continue to Worship; We Continue to Believe that the Best is yet to come!!

Scripture tells us that we must "Study to show ourselves Approved. The Affirmations on the pages of this book are written with one purpose alone. As you read each one, you will see yourself, and your struggles. You will hear your voice, and your cries. Most importantly, you will hear God's voice reminding you that you are Favored! Chosen! Hand Picked for your unique journey and that No one, and I do mean No one between here and hell can take from you what God has given. What has he given, hmm, I'm glad you asked? God gave the life of his only begotten Son so that you and I would not have to pay the price of disobedience. He gave us another opportunity to make better decisions in what we do with the gift of life that he bestowed upon us. He gave us the mere breath that we are breathing right now. He gave us Foundation. If we adhere to the instructions of Gods words, our life will never be void. His promise to us is that He will bless us abundantly, Press Down, Shaken Together, and Running Over. The visionary for this Blessed Work has seen her share of struggles, heartaches, and letdowns. Life screamed time and time again that she was not good enough for the abundance of God. Aren't we Glad she chose to hear God's voice over the enemy's tricks and lies? Angela Thomas Smith, thank you for being obedient to the assignment in which God is trusting you with. You have brought us All together on the foundation of God, and that my dear Sister is Christ, is the work of the Kingdom.

ACKNOWLEDGEMENT

I give honor to God my creator today for my very existence. It is by his strength that I can do all I do. So, I give him GLORY and PRAISE for just allowing this to be.

I honor my parents on today even in their absence their presence is felt daily. I thank God daily for every ounce of them that's been stirred up in me. GLEEN LEE THOMAS JR AND CATHERINE MARTIN THOMAS REST EASY, TRAVEL ON WE SHALL MEET AGAIN.

I want to thank every single QUEEN that took time to share an affirmation in this book. I SPEAK BLESSINGS OVER YOUR LIFE MAY EVERYTHING YOU TOUCH PROSPER IN JESUS NAME. We are the change we desire to see.

Special thanks to everyone that preorder the book WE LOVE YOU AND AINT NOTHING YOU CAN DO ABOUT IT. Our desire is that you will learn a little while showing some love as a leader for the kingdom of God. Pray this book blesses you and everyone you share it with. In Jesus name.

Angela Thomas Smith

OPENING PRAYER

✶✶✶✶✶✶✶✶✶✶

Father I bless you on today. Thanks for dropping this vision in my spirit. Thanks for each person attached to this project. I speak blessings over every person that shall pick this book up. My prayer is that the words will become life to them that read .

Father I declare and decree increase and overflow, every need shall be met. Father I thank you for watching over us as we try walk out this journey we call LIFE. Thanks for another chance to get it right.

This is my prayer I ask in Jesus name that your will be done. Amen Amen Amen ..

AFFIRMATION

WHATEVER HAPPENED BEFORE THIS VERY MOMENT IS NOW APART OF HISTORY ERASE IT.

L.E.A.R.N.   L.O.V.E.   L.E.A.D

LEARN

L- Less of me and more of God

E- Ego check, no room for feelings.

A- Ancestorial Anointing – faith and prayers of those that came before us (Spirits never die).

R- Resilience, your willingness to not give up. Pushing pass all that comes your way, true meaning of OVERCOMER.

N- Next Level in GOD. Know you have purpose you weren't dropped out the sky

I believe in myself and trust in my own wisdom. I am confident and capable in what I do. God Is Love

Cheniera Osbourne

God Is Making Room for Your Gift!

L.E.A.R.N.   L.O.V.E.   L.E.A.D

DAY # 1

Deuteronomy 4:27

King James Version

27 And the Lord shall scatter you among the nations, and ye shall be left few in number among the heathen, whither the Lord shall lead you.

■■■

PRAYER

I come before you, O Lord to say Thank You for another day.

AFFIRMATION

Dominique E. Jones

"I am whole. Anything I put my mind to I can and I will. My life is full of lessons and further then I was yesterday so i have a purpose

DAY #2

Judges 5:12

New International Version

[12] 'Wake up, wake up, Deborah!

Wake up, wake up, break out in song!

Arise, Barak!

Take captive your captives, son of Abinoam.'

PRAYER

****

Dear Lord, Thank You for fearfully and wonderfully creating

each of us.

AFFIRMATION

Bridget N. Tharpe

Words are bridges of life. With them my destiny is established. I erect the pillars of confidence. I believe in my abilities. I speak and claim my victory and success.

DAY #3

Psalm 5:8

New International Version

[8] Lead me, LORD, in your righteousness
because of my enemies—
make your way straight before me.

PRAYER

****

Lord Thank You for husbands, I give thanks for My Husband
Kent & Heal His Body Remove Anything That's Not Of You
In Jesus Name Amen

AFFIRMATION

Alexandria J. Garrett

Life is full of wolves that are
clothed in sheep clothing, but
the one who sustain my life is
Him who is the

Lamb of life.....the Bible.

DAY # 4

Psalm 25:5

New International Version

⁵ Guide me in your truth and teach me,

for you are God my Savior,

and my hope is in you all day long

■■

PRAYER

Father God Thank You For Angela And Pamela. True Women Of God Lord
Use Them In A Special Way Bless Their Home, Bless Their Family, Bless
Their Business In Jesus Name Amen.

AFFIRMATION

LaShone L. Grimes

POSITIVE AFFIRMATION

My beauty radiates on the inside.

God has created me to be
confident, strong, fearless and
courageous.

My future is bright and I'm
destined for greatness. I AM
WORTH IT!

DAY #5

Psalm 27:11

New International Version

[11] Teach me your way, LORD;

lead me in a straight path

because of my oppressors.

PRAYER

****

Father God Bless Your Land And Keep Your Arms Wrapped Around Your
People In Jesus Name Amen

AFFIRMATION

Shante Reed

Humble pie will never
leave you full.

Arrogance is gluttony.

DAY #6

Psalm 31:3

New International Version

[3] Since you are my rock and my fortress,
for the sake of your name lead and guide me..

PRAYER

****

Lord Thank You for my family Lord Watch Over Them and Bless Them In
A Special Way In Jesus Name Amen.

AFFIRMATION

Queashar L. Halliburton, Author

I am a legacy builder.

I am a courageous woman worthy of honor.

I will use my God-given gifts to make a global impact and change the lives of millions!

L.E.A.R.N.   L.O.V.E.   L.E.A.D

DAY # 7

Psalm 43:3

New International Version

³ Send me your light and your faithful care,
let them lead me;
let them bring me to your holy mountain,
to the place where you dwell.

PRAYER

****

.Father God Keep Your Loving Arms And Angels Around My Children
And Grandson Father God Keep Blessings My Children and Grandson In
Jesus Name Amen.

AFFIRMATION

Carolyn Annette Martin

Don't spend time worrying about things you have no control over. Be true to yourself.

19

DAY #8

Psalm 61:2

New International Version

[2] From the ends of the earth I call to you,

I call as my heart grows faint;

lead me to the rock that is higher than I.

PRAYER

****

Father God I Pray That You Keep Working on sons around the world, as

you work on my son Antonio. Father open the prison doors before

2022 and bring my son home to raise his son in Jesus name Amen.

****

AFFIRMATION

Author Kela Calvin

Lord, I thank you that I'm
alive. I don't take for granted
your grace and healing
mercies. I declare and decree
to live the healthy life that I
deserve, Amen.

DAY #9

Psalm 143:10

New International Version

[10] Teach me to do your will,

for you are my God;

may your good Spirit

lead me on level ground.

PRAYER

****

Father God work on those behind prison wall; please work on my Nephew
Elijah and remove them bar and give him a 2nd Chance At Life In Jesus
Name Amen

AFFIRMATION

Kashinda T. Marche

"I AM more than any
diagnosis that places a
barrier in my path toward
inner freedom

DAY # 10

Proverbs 8:20

New International Version

[20] I walk in the way of righteousness,
along the paths of justice

PRAYER

****

Lord Work On men around the world, as you work on My Nephew Larry
And Give Him A 2nd Chance At Life In Jesus Name Amen.

AFFIRMATION

La'mia Pierce

I am confident, I am strong and I am unstoppable in all my pursuits

DAY #11

Proverbs 6:22

New International Version

[22] When you walk, they will guide you;

when you sleep, they will watch over you;

when you awake, they will speak to you.

PRAYER

****

Father God Keep My natural Sisters Covered And Blessed, as well as my Sisters in Christ In Jesus Name Amen.

AFFIRMATION

Miranda Starks
Father, I thank you for the Supernatural gift of Joy! Because I delight myself in you, your Joy is my strength! Despite my circumstances, I Choose Joy!   In Jesus' Name, Amen

DAY #12

Isaiah 42:16

New International Version

[16] I will lead the blind by ways they have not known,

along unfamiliar paths I will guide them;

I will turn the darkness into light before them

and make the rough places smooth.

These are the things I will do;

I will not forsake them.

PRAYER

****

Lord Open Up Doors For your children Businesses around this world, In Jesus Name Amen.

AFFIRMATION

Shannan Starr
"Scrutiny, responsibility and honesty
are PRE-requisites for self-evolution. None of which are contingent upon external influences. Don't point the finger

L.E.A.R.N.   L.O.V.E.   L.E.A.D

DAY # 13

Isaiah 57:18

New International Version

[18] I have seen their ways, but I will heal them;
I will guide them and restore comfort to Israel's mourners,

PRAYER

****

Father God Continue To Work On Me And Show Me The Path That's In
Your Will Let It Be Done In Jesus Name Amen.

AFFIRMATION

Shannan Starr

"I see you Queen!
Healing unapologetically...
Without boundaries and unashamed...
Fermenting your right of speech with
complete sentences of "no" and "okay."
Organically unexplained...
Authentically loved by you!
Express yourself!" Organically unexplained...
Authentically loved by you!
Express yourself!"

DAY #14

Luke 6:39

New International Version

[39] He also told them this parable: "Can the blind lead the blind? Will they not both fall into a pit?

PRAYER

****

Father God Watch Over families around this world as you watch over, My Husband Family In Jesus Name Amen.

AFFIRMATION

Vernae Taylor

You are extraordinary! God formed you in your mother's womb and breathed PURPOSE into your life. God has designed a perfect plan for your future. So dare to LIVE.

DAY #15

Matthew 15:14

New International Version

[14] Leave them; they are blind guides.[a] If the blind lead the blind, both will fall into a pit."

PRAYER

****

Father God Thank You For The Ups And Downs The Storms The Good Days And Bad Days Lord Thank You In Jesus Name Amen.

AFFIRMATION

Chavonne D. Stewart

Sisters, we are Christ's masterpiece according to Ephesians 2:10 (NLT). Created in His image and clothed in his grace We are destined for greatness.

Matthew 6:13

New International Version

[13] And lead us not into temptation,[a]
but deliver us from the evil one.[b]'

■■■

PRAYER

Father God Thank You For Working On My Body And Removing The
Covid From Me and all your children around the world. Continue to line us
up to your will & way, In Jesus Name Amen

AFFIRMATION

Author Chantal Jennings

Change Relentless helping
and changing continuing
thing's in your life.

DAY #17

Revelation 7:17

New International Version

[17] For the Lamb at the center of the throne
will be their shepherd;
'he will lead them to springs of living water.'[a]
'And God will wipe away every tear from their eyes.'

PRAYER

****

Father God Continue To Bless Angela On Her Journey and lives of
everyone attached to this project. In Jesus Name Amen

AFFIRMATION

Tia Melvin

Poverty ends with me.
Wealth begins with me. I
create my own reality.

L.E.A.R.N.   L.O.V.E.   L.E.A.D

DAY #18

Psalm 23:3

New International Version

³   he refreshes my soul.
He guides me along the right paths
for his name's sake.

PRAYER

****

Lord, may nothing separate me from You today.

AFFIRMATION

Chyrel J. Jackson

You're very presence in any day makes the impossible; I'm Possible. Always know

God makes all things Possible.

DAY # 19

Jeremiah 29:13

New International Version

[13] You will seek me and find me when you seek me with all your heart.

PRAYER

****

Teach me how to choose only Your way today so each step will lead me closer to You.

AFFIRMATION

Lyris D. Wallace

1 John 4:4- greater is he that is in you, than he that is in the world.

DAY #20

Galatians 6:9

New International Version

[9] Let us not become weary in doing good, for at the proper time we will reap a harvest if we do not give up.

PRAYER

****

Father, help me walk by the Word and not my feelings.

AFFIRMATION

SR. Pastor Teresa S. McCurry

Leadership is the capacity to translate vision into reality.

It's about empowering others. "Authority by which the Christian leader leads is by love. Not force, intimidation, but reasoned encouragement ".

DAY #21

Philippians 2:3

New International Version

[3] Do nothing out of selfish ambition or vain conceit. Rather, in humility value others above yourselves,

PRAYER

****

Father, help me to keep my heart pure and undivided.

AFFIRMATION

Lakia Barnett

I Am Beautiful Inside And
Out
I Am The Woman God Called
Me To Be
I Am Strong
I Am Chosen
I Am Brave
I Am Proud To Be A Woman

DAY # 22

Philippians 4:13

New International Version

[13] I can do all this through him who gives me strength.

PRAYER

****

Father, protect me from my own careless thoughts, words, and actions.

AFFIRMATION

Savy Dawson
Flip the Switch

A person that turns the light on during darkness will always see the positive in adverse situations.
- "God is light; in him, there is no darkness at all." (1 John 1:5)

DAY #23

Proverbs 27:23

New International Version

[23] Be sure you know the condition of your flocks,
give careful attention to your herds;

PRAYER

****

Father, keep me from being distracted by MY wants, MY desires, MY thoughts on how things should be.

AFFIRMATION

Telecia Stanton

I have a purpose

I am perseverance

Failure is not an option

I hope that individuals' will overcome life daily challenges and stand with confidence as they walk in their truth and purpose that God's afforded to them.

L.E.A.R.N.   L.O.V.E.   L.E.A.D

DAY #24

Luke 6:31

New International Version

[31] Do to others as you would have them do to you.

PRAYER

****

Father, help me to embrace what comes my way as an opportunity... rather than a personal inconvenience.

AFFIRMATION

Arica P Quinn

Transformed Woman!
The beauty in the transformation of the caterpillar to the butterfly is not that it becomes a butterfly but that it can never return to being a caterpillar.

DAY # 25

Matthew 20:26

New International Version

[26] Not so with you. Instead, whoever wants to become great among you must be your servant,

PRAYER

****

Father, help me to rest in the truth of

Your Name

Amen.

AFFIRMATION

SR. Pastor Teresa S. McCurry

The Most powerful thing in the universe is LOVE !! True love is irresistible, when true love of God is presented no one can say no...It is like electricity.

DAY #26

Proverbs 29:11

New International Version

[11] Fools give full vent to their rage,

but the wise bring calm in the end

PRAYER

● ●

Father I thank you for wisdom, knowledge and understanding during this season. Keep me aligned with your word and will for my LIFE in Jesus name.

AFFIRMATION

Tando Tullia Keke

I am in covenant with integrity in my divine purpose, my soul, my creativity, and my ever-expanding capacity to sacrificially love others as a co-creator with God.

DAY #27

Luke 22:26

New International Version

[26] But you are not to be like that. Instead, the greatest among you should be like the youngest, and the one who rules like the one who serve.

PRAYER by Angela

****

Father today I am humbled because you saw fit to wake me up this morning. That alone I give you praise because you didn't have to.

AFFIRMATION

Author Joanne F Blake

I will always Promote, Push, and Prosper my way to the next level.

DAY # 28

Matthew 20:26

New International Version

²⁶ Not so with you. Instead, whoever wants to become great among you must be your servant,

■■

PRAYER by Angela

Father I thank you today because you have no respectable person what you do for one you will do for another. You said in Genesis 2:7 you breathe the breath of LIFE in us. A part of you always in me so I cant help but give you praise and honor so this day I just want to say thank you for keeping watch over us all.

AFFIRMATION

Pauline
Atkinson

I will share my talents.

DAY #29

Mark 9:35

New International Version

[35] Sitting down, Jesus called the Twelve and said, "Anyone who wants to be first must be the very last, and the servant of all."

PRAYER by Angela

****

Father today I come before you with thanksgiving. Thanking you for LIFE, HEALTH and STRENGTH. Father if you don't do another thing for me I will be forever grateful for what you have done. Thanks for awaken me to your truth and good new. AMEN

AFFIRMATION

SUSAN TURNER

I am striving to be the image of God. When you look at me I want you to see him.

DAY #30

Hebrews 13:7

New International Version

[7] Remember your leaders, who spoke the word of God to you. Consider the outcome of their way of life and imitate their faith.

PRAYER by Angela

****

Father no matter what come at me I will not be moved because I know what you have spoken to my spirit In JESUSNAME.   I will be all that you have purposed me to be.

IN JESUS NAME AMEN. AMEN. AMEN

■■■

AFFIRMATION

Annette Worwell

To thy own self be true

DAY # 31

Romans 1:1

New International Version

1 Paul, a servant of Christ Jesus, called to be an apostle and set apart for the gospel of God—

PRAYER by Angela

****

Father, I thank you for reminding me that you have given me POWER to be the best version of me I can be in your image. Father continue to guide and direct my every step. Father never let me think it's about me or anything that I have do. (I have no power. Father I thank you in Jesus name for loving me enough to bring me out the dark....

AFFIRMATION

JonQuil Medley

I am AMAZING
I am created in God's image
My past does not define me
My life IS a testimony
I am GRATEFUL for my wilderness

DAY #32

Matthew 20:28

New International Version

[28] just as the Son of Man did not come to be served, but to serve, and to give his life as a ransom for many."

PRAYER by Angela

****

Father thanks for creating me in your image. Father your word tells me I was fearfully and wonderfully made so today I gives thanks for being the apple of your EYE. Lead me in your righteousness and truth always. In Jesus Name this is my prayer.

AFFIRMATION

Clare Ezeakacha

I am one of a kind, I lead by love and deserve to be loved.

DAY #33

1 Timothy 4:12

New International Version

[12] Don't let anyone look down on you because you are young, but set an example for the believers in speech, in conduct, in love, in faith and in purity..

PRAYER by Angela

****

Father today I ask that you USE me to be an example to draw someone unto you today... Allow me to be a living TESTIMONY in Jesus name!

AFFIRMATION

Tammy Nicole Myers

When you have conquered certain theories of life experiences, it teaches you to prevail. Keep projecting the Spiritual fire out of your soul as God of Universe will permission it.

DAY # 34

2 Timothy 2:15

New International Version

[15] Do your best to present yourself to God as one approved, a worker who does not need to be ashamed and who correctly handles the word of truth.

PRAYER by Angela

****

Father thank you once again for breathing LIFE into me, Genesis 2:7 I thank you that your words shall not return to you void. You shall watch over it until its perfected in us and in this earth. Father I thank you in Jesus' name.

AFFIRMATION

Delicia Mayes R.T(R)(MR)
A small voice says "Pray!" The Holy Spirit is telling you to talk to God, your comforter, strengthener, protector, and healer. Fear not, the great I AM is with you! (Ish 41:10)

DAY #35

Mark 10:45

New International Version

[45] For even the Son of Man did not come to be served, but to serve, and to give his life as a ransom for many."

PRAYER by Angela

****

Father today I am reminded of the price JESUS paid for us all. Father thanks for thanking enough of us to send your son before us to show us the way. Father you said we shall do greater works. I stand on your word today. It shall not return to you void. In Jesus Name this my prayer. Amen. Amen. Amen

AFFIRMATION

Antoinette Osborn

In Genesis 1: 14 – 15, God separate seasons, like He separates people. Don't fear what the Creator is doing. What we see as seasons, God sees as training. We serve as a sign.

DAY #36

Isaiah 41:10

New International Version

[10] So do not fear, for I am with you;
do not be dismayed, for I am your God.
I will strengthen you and help you;
I will uphold you with my righteous right hand

PRAYER by Angela

****

**Father in JESUS name LET YOUR WILL BE DONE ALL
OVER THIS EARTH. EVERYONE THAT READS THIS
PASSAGE ON TODAY SHALL WALK IN VICTORY IN
YOU. THEIR LIVES WILL NEVER BE THE SAME. I
SPEAK WITH THE AUTHORITY OF THE HOLY SPIRIT
THAT WORKS IN ME THRU YOU. IN YOUR SON
JESUS NAME AMEN. AMEN. AMEN.**

AFFIRMATION

Angela Cole-Claiborne

My eyes are lifted up to
The One who gives me
help.

DAY # 37

John 3:30

New International Version

[30] He must become greater; I must become less.

PRAYER by Angela

****

Father thank you for yet another chance at LIFE to be a living example to help lead someone out of the darkness into the LIGHT. Father today if there is anything in me not like you or contrary to your word I ask in your son Jesus name to remove it from me. Father line me u with the path YOU have for my LIFE! This is my prayer. Amen. Amen. Amen

AFFIRMATION

Jessica Starks

God tailored your story just for you. Good, bad, and ugly - it was meant for you. Own it, embrace it, and use it to fulfill His purpose for your life.

DAY #38

Matthew 7:12

New International Version

[12] So in everything, do to others what you would have them do to you, for this sums up the Law and the Prophets.

PRAYER by Angela

****

Father if you abide in me (Genesis 2:7) then my LIFE should be a living example of your LOVE and everything I do shall be in love. What I give to the Universe shall return. Father allow me to be intentional about the things of you today and everyday going forth. In JESUS NAME.

AFFIRMATION

Kim Knight

Health, wealth, love, and prosperity surround me. My path ahead is blessed, and the road is open for even more success. Everything I envision is on its way to me.

DAY #39

Proverbs 4:23

New International Version

[23] Above all else, guard your heart,
for everything you do flows from it.

PRAYER by Angela

****

Father

**YOUR WILL BE DONE IN ME AND THRU ME ON
TODAY. KEEP MY MIND STAYED ON YOU! IN JESUS
NAME I PRAY. AMEN**

AFFIRMATION

Daphne Hampton
You matter everyday all day!

51

DAY # 40

Proverbs 29:2

New International Version

[2] When the righteous thrive, the people rejoice;
when the wicked rule, the people groan.

■■

PRAYER by Angela

**Father today I walk in your righteousness. As a believer I
must understand the POWER I possess thru you. Today
father I ask that you equip me with the wisdom to be in this
world but not of this world. Keep me on the path to
righteousness in Jesus' name.   AMEN**

■■

AFFIRMATION

Pastor Victoria L. Burse

I am an Apostolic Leader

I establish functioning
Apostolic Communities of
believers who are effective,
empowered, and skilled. We
engage in Divine purposes and
impact our Homes, Nations
and World.

DAY #41

Acts 20:28

New International Version

[28] Keep watch over yourselves and all the flock of which the Holy Spirit has made you overseers. Be shepherds of the church of God,[a] which he bought with his own blood

PRAYER by Angela

****

Father I plead the blood of Jesus over our lives. I believe in your word; it is the truth and the light. Align us that we may not stray. In Jesus name this is my prayer. Amen amen amen.

AFFIRMATION

Chioma Chigozie-Okwum

I am a queen, redeemed by the supernatural blood of the Lamb.

I am unstoppable, strong and resilient.

I am a winner, and my life is a testimonial.

I am an overcomer.

I am an inspiration to my world.

I am a pathfinder for my tribe

I am a warrior Queen because Christ lives in me..

DAY #42

Mark 9:42

New International Version

Causing to Stumble

[42] "If anyone causes one of these little ones—those who believe in me—to stumble, it would be better for them if a large millstone were hung around their neck and they were thrown into the sea.

PRAYER by Angela

Father remove me out the way and fill me with more of you on this day. Allow me to be a living example of your word. Your word reminds me that we are not to just listen and receive the word but be doers of the word. Father have your way in me in Jesus' name!!!

AFFIRMATION

Tabitha Stevens

You are a Proverbs 31 Woman. You are fearfully and wonderfully made: MARVELOUS are they works...says Ps139. In uncertainty be still and know that I am God. Amen

DAY # 43

Psalm 124:2

New International Version

² if the LORD had not been on our side
when people attacked us,

PRAYER by Angela

****

**Father I thank you I have POWER in your words and nothing can
come against that**

AFFIRMATION

Kadian Palmer-Asemota

I love my self
I love the person i am today
I love my testimonies from all my storms
I am loved and highly favored

DAY #44

Psalm 125:1

New International Version

[1] Those who trust in the LORD are like Mount Zion,
which cannot be shaken but endures forever.

PRAYER by Angela

****

**Father today I stand on your word, your truth and I shall not
be moved. No matter what it looks like in the natural I know
that you have already worked it in the spirit so today I walk
in victory in you! Amen Amen Amen**

■■

AFFIRMATION

Malik Beckett

I'm no longer a slave to
my pain but a master in
this win of understanding
what is for me. I'm
actually at peace, and
God play a major part of
my happiness.

DAY #45

Psalm 127:1

New International Version

[1] Unless the LORD builds the house,
the builders labor in vain.
Unless the LORD watches over the city,
the guards stand watch in vain.

PRAYER by Angela

****

Father today I thank you for every woman attached to this project. Father I ask that you strengthen each of them in all areas they may be weak in. Father give us the will to endure and not all hinderances to keep us bond when your word already tells me I am free.

AFFIRMATION

Tamara M. Singleton

I am not my mistakes; I am worthy of acceptance, love, and prosperity

DAY # 46

Psalm 122:1

New International Version

[1] I rejoiced with those who said to me,
"Let us go to the house of the LORD."

PRAYER by Angela

****

Father today I give you praise for allowing me another chance to get it right. Another chance to impact someone's life. You have given us some many gifts and talents to bring change and healing to your people and the land. Today father I ask you to stir each dormant gift; that we may be a light to someone's dark path

AFFIRMATION

Sr. Pastor Teresa S. McCurry

We have to consider the impact our words can have on other people. God created us to be passionate beings, and our words hold the power of life

DAY #47

Psalm 128:1

New International Version

[1] Blessed are all who fear the LORD,
who walk in obedience to him.

PRAYER by Angela

****

Today I thank you father for truly showing me what the word LIFE meant, without Love how could I Inspire someone to come out of the darkness. Having the true FEAR of God that reminds me why me why I am here in the first place; to be an example of the E3EXPERIENCE (educate, empower, and encourage) others into the LIGHT(TRUTH). Father today don't allow LIFE to happen around me ALLOW me to be A part of LIFE.

AFFIRMATION

Valerie Young
Virtuous Woman- A
Queen tailored for my
king
Blessed- Grateful for the
small things: mustard
seed
I am Valerie: I'm on a
spiritual journey having a
human experience as
Valerie Young

DAY #48

Psalm 120:1

New International Version

[1] I call on the LORD in my distress,
and he answers me.

PRAYER by Angela

****

Father today I cast all my cares upon you. Thou will be done on this day in Jesus' name. Amen

****

AFFIRMATION

Tonya. L. Vernon

Love is patient, love is kind. It does not envy, it does not boast, It is not proud. It does not dishonor others, it is not self-serving, it is not easily angered. 1 Corinthians 13:4-8.

Loving God and yourselves and others will pay off after while. Be encouraged.

DAY #49

PSALM 134

NEW INTERNATIONAL VERSION

[1] Praise the LORD, all you servants of the LORD

who minister by night in the house of the LORD.

[2] Lift up your hands in the sanctuary

and praise the LORD.

[3] May the LORD bless you from Zion,

he who is the Maker of heaven and earth

PRAYER by Angela

****

Father today I yield to be used by you. Your will not mines in Jesus' name I pray. Amen

AFFIRMATION

Elder Barbara Brown-Stewart
I am more than a Conqueror and an upgrade by God..."waiting to happen to something or someone"

DAY #50

PSALM 130:1-2

NEW INTERNATIONAL VERSION

[1] Out of the depths I cry to you, *LORD*;
[2]   Lord, hear my voice.
Let your ears be attentive
to my cry for mercy.

PRAYER by Angela

****

FATHER MY PRAYER TODAY IS THAT YOU HEAR OUR PRAYERS AND ANSWER THEM ACCORDING TO YOUR WILL FOR OUR LIVES. LINE US UP TODAY TO RECEIVE YOUR TRUTH IN JESUS NAME.

AFFIRMATION

Shana Gourdine

The H is for Helping

The E is for Empower

The A is for Ambitious

The L is for Leaders

When you have been through a storm, we have to member that our situations are not about us. We go through the trials and tribulations to be able to heal the other individual that we are assigned to help them through their purpose

DAY # 51

Proverbs 1:5

NEW INTERNATIONAL VERSION

⁵ let the wise listen and add to their learning,
and let the discerning get guidance

PRAYER

****

Father today allow me to Forget what is behind and reaching forward
to what is ahead . Father this is my prayer on today. I am reminded of
Philippians 3:13 "Brothers, I do not consider myself to have taken
hold of it. But one thing I do: Forgetting what is behind and reaching
forward to what is ahead."

AFFIRMATION

LISA HAYES

I am confident. I am beautiful. I am smart and I am enough.

DAY #52

PROVERBS 3:1

NEW INTERNATIONAL VERSION

My son, do not forget my teaching,

but keep my commands in your heart,

PRAYER
■■■

Father I ask that you give me wisdom on today. Father guide and lead
in the path of righteousness. Father allow me to have compassion for
your people (Proverbs 10:23 "Doing wickedness is like sport to a fool,
and so is wisdom to a man of understanding).

AFFIRMATION

Terrie Sylvester
With Jesus I'm Unstoppable
When I take a shot it's nothing
but net
"Whoosh" 3 pointers all day
*I   can   do
all things through Christ   who
strengthens me. Phil 4:13*

DAY #53

PROVERBS 6:22

NEW INTERNATIONAL VERSION

²² When you walk, they will guide you;

when you sleep, they will watch over you;

when you awake, they will speak to you

PRAYER

****

Lord, I Thank You For Waking Me Up This Morning Giving Me
Another Day To Get It Right. Allow your will to be done thru me
today. This my prayer in Jesus' name. Your will not mines amen
amen amen.

■■

AFFIRMATION

Dr. LaDonna Hollis

I am appreciating the gift of wisdom as I work on my future self.

DAY # 54

PROVERBS 9:10

NEW INTERNATIONAL VERSION

[10] The fear of the LORD is the beginning of wisdom,

and knowledge of the Holy One is understanding.

PRAYER

****

Keep Working On Me Change My Heart To Your Ways Lord. I Pray

For My Husband Kent Osbourne, My Daughters Vonterkia Collins,

L'sha Roberts And My Son Antonio Roberts, My Grandson Asthon

Roberts and all the families that's connected to this project. Father I

ask That You Watch Over Them In Jesus Name Amen.

AFFIRMATION

Charlotte Simon

A wise builder will build on the surety of the words of God which last forever whereas a foolish builder will build on whatever is new for the moment.

DAY #55

Proverbs 13:1

New International Version

13 A wise son heeds his father's instruction,
but a mocker does not respond to rebukes.'

PRAYER

****

Father I'm asking if there is Anything That's Not Of You Remove It
Right Now In Jesus Name Amen.

AFFIRMATION

Pastor Tamela Lucus

Were taught to love everyone. We have to learn how to love ourselves first. We need to stop punishing ourselves by saying we don't deserve anything good.

DAY #56

PROVERBS 16:3

NEW INTERNATIONAL VERSION

³ Commit to the *LORD* whatever you do,
and he will establish your plans.

PRAYER

****

Lord Keep My Parents and all the Parents around the world safe In
Your Hands And Watch Over Them In Jesus Name Amen.

■■

AFFIRMATION

Tasha Downing

I am love.

I am purpose.

I was made with
divine intention.

DAY # 57

PROVERBS 18:21

NEW INTERNATIONAL VERSION

[21] The tongue has the power of life and death,
and those who love it will eat its fruit.

PRAYER

**Father I am grateful today, Lord, you woke me up and you didn't
have to. You allowed me to be in my right mind. You allowed me
to speak your truth and your word. I give you praise on today.,
you are worthy of all my praise in JESUS name.**

∎∎

AFFIRMATION

Cheryl LeGrand

I can do all things
through Christ who
strengthens me

69

DAY #58

PROVERBS 20:11

NEW INTERNATIONAL VERSION

[11] Even small children are known by their actions,
so is their conduct really pure and upright?

PRAYER

****

I Pray That You Move in A Special Way. Heal The Sick, Watch Over
Your Homeless People. Jesus Watch Over All My Sisters & Brothers
Open Doors Up For Them.

AFFIRMATION

Minister Renita Singleton
The Power in Purpose
There's Power in Your Purpose!
It Encompasses the Power to
Love, for Healing, to Overcome!
Your Purpose Enables You to do
All that Jesus did and Greater!

DAY #59

PROVERBS 25:28

NEW INTERNATIONAL VERSION

[28] Like a city whose walls are broken through
is a person who lacks self-control.

PRAYER by Angela

****

**Father I thank you for yet another day to give you praise. Teach
me how to be slow to anger and how to demonstrate love in all I do
in your son Jesus name.**

AFFIRMATION

Tiara Snyder
Affirmation words,
the POWER to
Speak & Manifest
things ...
Profession
Declaration
Insistence
Confirmation

DAY # 60

PROVERBS 27:1

NEW INTERNATIONAL VERSION

27 Do not boast about tomorrow,
for you do not know what a day may bring.

PRAYER by Angela

****

**Father keep me humble, courageous, and bold. Today I ask you
line me up with your plan for my LIFE. Remove me out of the
way; stir up those gifts and talents that's inside of me. This is my
prayer today, may your will be done all around this world.**

AFFIRMATION

Courageous Diva
Barbara Palmer
DARE TO LIVE
BOLDLY!
You are never too old to
follow your dreams!

DAY #61

ISAIAH 54:17

NEW INTERNATIONAL VERSION

[17] no weapon forged against you will prevail,

and you will refute every tongue that accuses you.

This is the heritage of the servants of the LORD,

and this is their vindication from me,"

declares the LORD.

PRAYER by Angela

****

Today I stand on your word. Father thank you for allowing me to see another day that was not promised me. Keep me humbled and steadfast on your word. In Jesus name amen.

AFFIRMATION

Cheryl Jones

I AM beautiful and wonderfully made. I AM strong and gifted. I AM loved . I AM who God says I am and I will not fell. I AM Blessed

DAY #62

PROVERBS 26:11-12

NEW INTERNATIONAL VERSION

[11] As a dog returns to its vomit,

so fools repeat their folly.

[12] Do you see a person wise in their own eyes?

There is more hope for a fool than for them.

PRAYER by Angela

****

Father keep me intentional about the things of you. Father never allow me to think it's about me or that someone owes me something. Father I just give you worship on today because you allowed me to awake with a right mind that's stayed on you.

AFFIRMATION

Dr. Kimberly Thomas

I am fearfully and wonderfully made in the glorious image of my creator. Though I have been broken, beaten, battered, cracked and chipped, I am still dipped in Destiny

74

DAY# 63

2 PETER 2:22

NEW INTERNATIONAL VERSION

[22] Of them the proverbs are true: "A dog returns to its vomit,"[a] and, "A sow that is washed returns to her wallowing in the mud."

PRAYER by Angela

****

FATHER YOU SAID YOU KNOW THE PLANS YOU HAVE FOR ME TO GIVE ME HOPE. FATHER YOU SAID IF I SEEK, I SHALL FIND, TODAY I SEEK YOU MY FATHERKEEP ME IN YOUR WILL, MORE OF YOU AND LESS OF ME IN JESUS NAME.

AFFIRMATION

Donna Garey
Know God, Know Peace. No God, No Peace.

DAY #64

PHILIPPIANS 3:13

NEW INTERNATIONAL VERSION

[13] Brothers and sisters, I do not consider myself yet to have taken hold of it. But one thing I do: Forgetting what is behind and straining toward what is ahead,

PRAYER by Angela

****

Father keep me stayed on you, let me not be moved no matter what comes my way. Father I trust your word and I know it shall not return to you void.   Father no matter what I face in this natural realm I will not stop striving for the things of the spirit. Keep me in your will father LEAD ME.

****

AFFIRMATION

Marcia Harton

. In him do I live move and have my being, for I AM nothing without you. Keep me ever so   close to you order my steps according to your word.

L.E.A.R.N.   L.O.V.E.   L.E.A.D

DAY #65

REVELATION 3:19

NEW INTERNATIONAL VERSION

[19] Those whom I love I rebuke and discipline. So be earnest and
repent.

PRAYER by Angela

****

**Father today I thank you for everyone that's reading this
devotional. Father, I thank you that they didn't think it
robbery to sow into this project. Father send a special
blessing to every person that purchased this book in FAITH.
Father stretch their faith on today.**

AFFIRMATION

Marcia Harton

Heavenly father in your
presence is where I want to
be. I worship, love and
adore you. I thank you for
the anointing. Use me for
your glory

DAY # 66

PROVERBS 12:15

NEW INTERNATIONAL VERSION

[15] The way of fools seems right to them,
but the wise listen to advice.

PRAYER by Angela

****

**Father I give you praise no matter what. If you don't do
another thing, I thank you because you have already do
enough, you woke me up and started me on my way. So, I
give you praise on today!! Amen Amen amen ..**

AFFIRMATION

Marcia Harton

Lord I come before you giving
you thanks for all the
wonderful things that you have
done and will continue to do
in my life. I need you always.

78

DAY #67

PROVERBS 18:15

NEW INTERNATIONAL VERSION

[15] The heart of the discerning acquires knowledge,
for the ears of the wise seek it out.

PRAYER by Angela

****

**Father I thank you for yet another day to bring you Glory
and honor. Father you didn't have to wake us up today,
but you did and we thank you. Father I thank you for
allowing the us the opportunity to make our petition
know onto you. Continue to bring me under your
submission in Jesus' name I pray.**

AFFIRMATION

Marcia Harton

Lord you are first in my life.
Enlarge my territory allow my
light to shine unto nations.

Keep me humble no matter how
you make my name great.
Amen.

DAY #68

LUKE 2:40

NEW INTERNATIONAL VERSION

[40] And the child grew and became strong; he was filled with wisdom, and the grace of God was on him.

PRAYER by Angela

****

Father keep me humble and teachable. Father in all of my learning never allow me to think it's about me. Father I thank you for how you are lining us all up to your word. Thank you for each person that will read this entry today. Father , today I walk in your purpose on purpose In your son Jesus Name!!!!!!

AFFIRMATION

Voncille Morton

Instead of trying to make yourself fit in, allow yourself space to stretch out.

DAY # 69

1 PETER 2:2-3

NEW INTERNATIONAL VERSION

[2] Like newborn babies, crave pure spiritual milk, so that by it you may grow up in your salvation, [3] now that you have tasted that the Lord is good

■■

PRAYER by Angela

Father today remove me out of the way, allow your spirit to speak thru me. Father today my prayer is that you will keep me holy and sanctified. Father allow my LIFE to be a living example at how to be a leader in Jesus' name this is my prayer.

AFFIRMATION

ELDER KIMBERLY MOORE

I AM WHO GOD SAYS I AM

I AM COURGEOUS

I AM RESILIENT, STRONG & BRILLANT

I AM ABLE TO GIVE LOVE BECAUSE OF SELF-LOVE

I CHOOSE FORGIVENESS, I CHOOSE LOVE

L.E.A.R.N.   L.O.V.E.   L.E.A.D

DAY #70

PROVERBS 3:1

NEW INTERNATIONAL VERSION

Wisdom Bestows Well-Being

3 My son, do not forget my teaching,
but keep my commands in your heart,

PRAYER by Angela

****

Father guard my heart today. Father keep those things that come to hinder me away on today. Father stir up the strengthen on the inside of me I may resist the enemy. Father I thank you for going before me and smooth out every crooked road. Father this is my prayer in Jesus name.

AFFIRMATION

Jane Hamick

Love is an action, not just words. Love has to be shown and expressed.

You can learn anything if you have the will and mindset to do so.

82

L.E.A.R.N. L.O.V.E. L.E.A.D

DAY #71

PROVERBS 4:5

NEW INTERNATIONAL VERSION

[5] Get wisdom, get understanding;
do not forget my words or turn away from them.

PRAYER by Angela

****

Father don't allow me to get so consumed with the things of this world that I forget you. Father never allow me to put anything before you. Remind me constantly why I even exist. Father today I father I ask you to watch over those that are homeless and have no place to call home. Father touch their mind and heart that they too may come out the dark into the marvelous light of Jesus Christ the only way to the father.

AFFIRMATION

Shiyla Nix

I don't have to prove who I am because I know who I am. I am who God says I am.

DAY # 72

PHILIPPIANS 4:9

NEW INTERNATIONAL VERSION

[9] Whatever you have learned or received or heard from me, or seen in me—put it into practice. And the God of peace will be with you.

PRAYER by Angela

****

Father today I lift those that are battle terminal illness. Father where man say NO you father says all things are possible!! We trust your word and your will for each of our lives. Father today I stand in the gap for that one that think they must be perfect or have to say certain words. Father I thank you for you knew my need before I even came. And I thank you for working it out right now in Jesus' name.

AFFIRMATION

Karen Kennedy
"God is bigger than my problems. He makes a way where there is no way. He is the light in the darkness. He hears me when I pray."

DAY #73

PSALM 32:8

NEW INTERNATIONAL VERSION

[8] I will instruct you and teach you in the way you should go;
I will counsel you with my loving eye on you.

PRAYER by Angela

****

Father thank you for just allowing me to be free.

Free to LEARN

Free to LOVE

Free to LEAD

AND

FREE TO SERVE YOU! In Jesus name, amen.

AFFIRMATION

Glendora Dvine LPC NCC

As we travel on our journey of life don't forget that life is short. We only have one life, we must live, don't just exist. Keep it moving!

DAY #74

1 THESSALONIANS 5:11

NEW INTERNATIONAL VERSION

[11] Therefore encourage one another and build each other up, just as in fact you are doing.

PRAYER by Angela

****

Father thanks for reminding me that I am who you created it me to be. I thank you for the spirit of a servant, the will to serve others and encourage them into their purpose. Lord, I thank you right now for the spirit of collaborations. Father never let me forget about why you allow me to exist.

AFFIRMATION

Kim C Rice

We have to learn to love ourselves. I spent many years loving someone that really did not know how to truly love others. Material things are not love. Now I am embarking on a journey that God Himself has prepared me. I did not understand why me, but God has showed me "Why Not Me?"

DAY # 75

PROVERBS 1:7

NEW INTERNATIONAL VERSION

[7] The fear of the LORD is the beginning of knowledge,

but fools[a] despise wisdom and instruction.

PRAYER by Angela

****

Father today renew, reset, and restore me to the path you have for me. Father forgive me for anything, that I have or will do that's out of your will. Lord if I fall, please don't allow me to stay down.

AFFIRMATION

Mattie Daniels

Transformed by the power of God's Love.

Romans

12:2.		Voices
	living inside my head.	Voices I longed to put to
bed.	"Unloving, poor, black,that's me"	God's Love. His
Beauty.	Transformed renewed.	Reading
	God's Word	You will be too.

DAY #76

PSALM 25:4

NEW INTERNATIONAL VERSION

[4] Show me your ways, LORD,
teach me your paths.

PRAYER by Angela

****

Your way father

Abba lead me on today.

Not my will but your will in Jesus name. amen

AFFIRMATION

Destiny Stanford

Despite what is handed to us in life, we have to learn how to use what we got and be happy. I'm deaf and beautiful.

DAY #77

PSALM 25:5

NEW INTERNATIONAL VERSION

⁵ Guide me in your truth and teach me,
for you are God my Savior,
and my hope is in you all day long.

PRAYER by Angela

****

Father in the name of Jesus I come before you right now asking that remove me out of the way and allow your glory to shine thru me. Father anything that is contrary to your word or not like you Lord I'm asking you to remove it right now . Father allow someone to see you in me on today. Let not my journey be about me but about a life I can touch in Jesus name AMEN...

AFFIRMATION

Laura Worthy-Crawford

Learn

Learn from your mistakes and do not let your past make you. God has already given us the victory when he sent us his son Jesus. Do not lose heart. 2 Corinthians 4:16-18

DAY #78

PROVERBS 12:1

NEW INTERNATIONAL VERSION

12 Whoever loves discipline loves knowledge,
but whoever hates correction is stupid

PRAYER by Angela

****

Father Today I lift every business, ministry, marriage, organization, family, and person attached to this movement and what God is doing thru us in this book. No weapon formed **against you shall prosper and every tongue that rises shall be condemned in Jesus name. Your will for our lives. I thank you for this journey keep filling us will more of you Father and I will always give you praise. Amen.**

AFFIRMATION

Janice Mayes

Cancer, Stroke, Open Heart Surgery but God kept me here! No matter what comes your way, as long as God is on your side you can do it!

DAY #79

DEUTERONOMY 8:5

NEW INTERNATIONAL VERSION

[5] Know then in your heart that as a man disciplines his son, so the LORD your God disciplines you.

PRAYER by Angela

****

Father I thank you for every prayer warrior that didn't think it robbery to be a part of this project and to allow you to speak thru them. Father today I ask that you give them strength when they feel weak. Father wrap your loving arms around your people. Father some are seeking for one thing, and some are seeking for another but Father you know all about us before we even come to you. Bless according to your will in JESUS name.

AFFIRMATION

Sharon Randolph

I am Black Beautiful. I am Lovable. I am Phenomenal. I am Enough. I am Resilient. I am Necessary. I am a Queen. I am Redeemed. I am Holy. I am Purpose. I am Loved.

L.E.A.R.N.   L.O.V.E.   L.E.A.D

ACTS 20:20

NEW INTERNATIONAL VERSION

[20] You know that I have not hesitated to preach anything that would be helpful to you but have taught you publicly and from house to house.

PRAYER by Angela

****

Father I thank you because I will WIN, I will win, I will WIN….. I am a champion, Father everything attached to me shall win. Father it's my winning SEASON. Father I thank you in Jesus' name

■■

AFFIRMATION

Tina Michelle Baker"

Just be you and watch God work through you!" EtB

DAY #81

LUKE 2:40

NEW INTERNATIONAL VERSION

[40] And the child grew and became strong; he was filled with wisdom, and the grace of God was on him.

PRAYER by Angela

****

Father I speak against that spirit of lack right now. Father your word said we are the head and not the tail, we have not because we ask not. Father I am asking you to lose supernatural abundance and overflow that we may be the lender and not the borrower. Father line us up that we may be a blessing to the kingdom for the building of the kingdom.

AFFIRMATION

Deborah Ivey

You can do it. Don't let them tell you that you can't. You can do anything when you put your mind to it.

Let me know if you need anything else from me.

93

DAY #82

PROVERBS 4:2

NEW INTERNATIONAL VERSION

[2] I give you sound learning,
so do not forsake my teaching

PRAYER by Angela

****

**Father today keep me humble, remove me out of the way. Allow
your word to be a lamp for my feet, a light on this path. Father
lead and direct my every step. Let me not get weary in well doing
but faint not and see what the end shall be in Jesus' name. He will
never lead us astray. Amen Amen Amen**

■■

AFFIRMATION

Qualisha K Benson

: "Our problems cannot be
solved at the same level of
thinking we were at when
we created them. Meditate
on this principle for
GROWTH!

94

DAY # 83

PROVERBS 9:9

NEW INTERNATIONAL VERSION

[9] Instruct the wise and they will be wiser still;
teach the righteous and they will add to their learning.

PRAYER by Angela

****

**Father keep us humble and seeking your truth. You are the only
way to the light. I'll trust you when I can't see you. I'll trust you
when I can't trace you. Father your word shall not return to you
void regardless of what it looks like in the natural. In Jesus name I
pray . Amen**

■■

AFFIRMATION

Ollie Thompson

Beautiful black woman of the sun, created by God. Lovingly speak peace, love and admiration to yourself. Be kind, positive and honor yourself....You are created, talented and ageless!

DAY #84

TITUS 2:1

NEW INTERNATIONAL VERSION

2 You, however, must teach what is appropriate to sound doctrine.

PRAYER by Angela

****

Father I thank you because your word reminds me that you are not slack concerning your promise. My prayer today is that thee will be done in our lives. Father watch over the homeless, those in hospitals, those in nursing homes, those in prison and those in mental institutions father touch their hearts, minds and soul speak to them and let them know they are not alone in Jesus name. Amen.

AFFIRMATION

Temekia Glenn

We must believe that God have a plan for our life. The only way to stay at God's feet is surrender your all through the good and the bad, whether you happy or sad, through the storm and the rain. My prayer is "God send the rain and shower us with your love. Roman 5;6-8

L.E.A.R.N.   L.O.V.E.   L.E.A.D

DAY #85

PROVERBS 22:6

NEW INTERNATIONAL VERSION

⁶ Start children off on the way they should go,
and even when they are old they will not turn from it.

PRAYER by Angela

****

Jesus

**The sweets name I know. Father thank you for sending your son
Jesus to be an example in the flesh. Today I thank you for your
word say we shall do greater works. Father I ask that today you
stir up that gift that Will SET THE KINGDOM ON FIRE. Father
I thank you for setting order all around the world in JESUS name.
AMEN**

AFFIRMATION

Nia Murdock

Every morning look at
yourself in the mirror
and say out loud,
Good morning
beautiful, I Love
You!! Self Love is the
best love.

L.E.A.R.N.   L.O.V.E.   L.E.A.D

DAY # 86

ROMANS 15:4

NEW INTERNATIONAL VERSION

[4] For everything that was written in the past was written to teach us, so
that through the endurance taught in the Scriptures and the
encouragement they provide we might have hope.

****

PRAYER by Angela

Father

Your will for me today father.

In Jesus name

AFFIRMATION
■■

Carmaria Cocoa Fenton
You are more than enough, you are an
overcomer and a conqueror!
Overcomer- To succeed in dealing with a
problem or difficulty and to prevail.
Conqueror- to overcome and take control of
a thing
You will and you shall live to see the
promises of God attached to your life
manifest. You can and you shall be Great!
Now remember this your atmosphere is
pregnant with purpose, grab hold and
PUSH!! Your Time and Your Season is
NOW!!

DAY #87

PROVERBS 10:7

NEW INTERNATIONAL VERSION

[7] The name of the righteous is used in blessings,[a]
but the name of the wicked will rot.

PRAYER by Angela

****

**Father forgive me of any sins I may have committed knowing
or not knowing, Let the mediation of my heart be acceptable
in thee sight. Renew a right spirit in me right now in Jesus'
name.**

AFFIRMATION

Chinyelu Uduchukwu-Akpaka

Learn
To Learn is to live
Learning is the air
To breathe you have to learn

To Learn is to know
Without knowledge
Living is meaningless

To learn is to conquer

PSALM 32:8

NEW INTERNATIONAL VERSION

[8] I will instruct you and teach you in the way you should go;
I will counsel you with my loving eye on you

PRAYER by Angela

****

**Father I plead the blood of Jesus over everyone attached to
this book and movement. Father no weapon formed against
them will prosper and every tongue that tries to rise will be
cut out from the root. Father I thank you because you have
given us Power to be an overcomer thru our resilience. These
tests came to make us strong, and I thank you for endurance
not giving up. In Jesus name. Amen**

AFFIRMATION

Samantha j. Jackson

When the Road seems long I
will believe in Myself to move
forward in Life, when the
leaves seems Brown I will
Blossom enough for the world
to see. I am Blessed, I am
Strong and I am God's
Masterpiece. I am a

Woman who will be
Empowered.

DAY # 89

JAMES 1:5

NEW INTERNATIONAL VERSION

[5] If any of you lacks wisdom, you should ask God, who gives generously to all without finding fault, and it will be given to you.

PRAYER by Angela

****

Father I thank you for a fresh anointing, fill me lord. Remove me out the way. Less of me and more of you in Jesus' name AMEN.

AFFIRMATION

Nakia Bradley

You are necessary. You are valuable. You are validated. You are loved. You require what you require. You matter. Let no one, not even you, tell you otherwise

DAY #90

JOHN 14:26

NEW INTERNATIONAL VERSION

[26] But the Advocate, the Holy Spirit, whom the Father will send in my name, will teach you all things and will remind you of everything I have said to you

PRAYER by Angela

****

Father today shower down a special blessing upon your people and I will be sure to give you praise. In Jesus name Amen.

AFFIRMATION

Aquintas Jones

I love me in spite of every circumstance I have faced and will face. I will not lose myself in my situations. My circumstances do not define me. I am loveable.

L.E.A.R.N.   L.O.V.E.   L.E.A.D

DAY #91

MATTHEW 28:19-20

NEW INTERNATIONAL VERSION

[19] Therefore go and make disciples of all nations, baptizing them in the name of the Father and of the Son and of the Holy Spirit, [20] and teaching them to obey everything I have commanded you. And surely I am with you always, to the very end of the age."

PRAYER by Angela

****

FATHER YOUR WILL FOR MY LIFE, I UNDERSTAND THIS LIFE IS NOT MINES BUT FOR THE BUILDING OF THE KINGDOM AND I THANK YOU IN JESUS NAME AMEN.

****

AFFIRMATION

Blaque Diamond

The invitation of peace is always there from Jesus. He will see me through it because he is the source of my peace for I trust him. Thank you for loving me enough and for granting me a new start in Jesus' name, Amen

DAY # 92

PSALM 25:4

NEW INTERNATIONAL VERSION

⁴ Show me your ways, LORD,
teach me your paths.

PRAYER by Angela

****

Father I thank you for your word today because you remind me that I may find peace in you. You also assured me that I would have tribulations, but you reminded me to be of good cheer because you have overcome the world. Thank you for making a way for me. In Jesus name amen.

AFFIRMATION

Blaque Diamond

The night before His crucifixion Jesus gave His disciples an amazing promise: "Peace I leave you, My peace I give you; not as the world gives, do I give to you. Do not let your hearts be troubled, nor fearful." (John 14:27).

DAY #93

1 CORINTHIANS 13:4-5

NEW INTERNATIONAL VERSION

[4] Love is patient, love is kind. It does not envy, it does not boast,
it is not proud. [5] It does not dishonor others, it is not self-
seeking, it is not easily angered, it keeps no record of wrongs.

PRAYER by Angela

****

**Father I thank you that today I can LOVE more and
understand what that word truly means. I learned on this
journey Love also covers a multitude of SIN.**

■■■

AFFIRMATION

Shelia C. Lewis

**Follow Your
Soul, It knows
the Way.**

DAY #94

1 CORINTHIANS 13:6-8

NEW INTERNATIONAL VERSION

[6] Love does not delight in evil but rejoices with the truth. [7] It always protects, always trusts, always hopes, always perseveres.

[8] Love never fails. But where there are prophecies, they will cease; where there are tongues, they will be stilled; where there is knowledge, it will pass away.

PRAYER by Angela

****

Father I thank you for the blood of JESUS. I plead the blood over my life and the lives of those attached to me. I can't thank you enough for life health and strength. Father watch over every area of our lives that we maybe example for the building of the kingdom of God. This is my prayer in Jesus name .amen.

AFFIRMATION

MAMA FORBES

It's nice to be old, but it's better to live to be old.

DAY # 95

1 JOHN 4:7-9

NEW INTERNATIONAL VERSION

7 Dear friends, let us love one another, for love comes from God.
Everyone who loves has been born of God and knows
God. 8 Whoever does not love does not know God, because God
is love. 9 This is how God showed his love among us: He sent
his one and only Son into the world that we might live through
him.

PRAYER by Angela

****

**Father build us up where we have been torn down. Give us
strength where we are weak. Father build a hedge of
protection around us keep all hurt harm or danger from
coming near us . In Jesus name I speak he blood of Jesus.**

AFFIRMATION

MAMA FORBES

Wisdom belongs to the aged, and understanding to the **old**. Grandchildren are the crown of the aged, and the glory of children is their fathers. Moses was 120 years **old** when he died, yet his eyesight was clear, and he was as strong as ever. Those who are older should **speak**, for wisdom comes with age.

L.E.A.R.N.   L.O.V.E.   L.E.A.D

ROMANS 5:8

NEW INTERNATIONAL VERSION

[8] But God demonstrates his own love for us in this: While we were still sinners, Christ died for us.

PRAYER by Angela

****

Father your will not mines. I thank you for allowing me to see another day, to share your goodness.

■■

AFFIRMATION

MAMA FORBES

Now that I am old and my hair is gray, don't leave me, God. I must tell the next generation about your power and greatness. God, your goodness reaches far above the skies. You have done wonderful things. God, there is no one like you.
~ Psalm 71:18-19

DAY #97

1 JOHN 3:18

NEW INTERNATIONAL VERSION

[18] Dear children, let us not love with words or speech but with actions and in truth.

PRAYER by Angela

****

Father today my prayer is that every door that needs to be open in the lives of those attached to this project in some way shape or form be opened in your son Jesus name. And every door that needs to be closed be shut right now in JESUS name. No weapon shall prosper AMEN.

AFFIRMATION

Marcia Harton

Make our request known unto you. There is nothing too hard for you. Jesus heal our bodies and make us whole. You are indeed a miracle worker. Jehovah Rapha.

DAY # 98

PROVERBS 10:12

NEW INTERNATIONAL VERSION

[12] Hatred stirs up conflict,
but love covers over all wrongs.

■■■

PRAYER by Angela

**Father I thank you for the spirit of LOVE that covers all sin.
Forgive us for we have fallen short of your glory. Father
keep me humble and steadfast on your word. Never let it be
about me. Remind me of this journey. In all things you
allow me to Learn, love and lead while serving the kingdom.
This is my prayer in Jesus' name.**

■■■

AFFIRMATION

Marcia Harton

I lift our children up to
you now. Keep your
hands all around them.
You abide in them and
they abide in you. Keep
them on the right path.

110

DAY #99

1 Corinthians 16:14

New International Version

[14] Do everything in love.

PRAYER by Angela

****

Father I thank you that even when the enemy try to come you always show me who you are and that your POWER is SUPERIOR AND NO OTHER POWER IS GREATER. Father I thank you for your word in Jesus' name.

■■

AFFIRMATION

Marcia Harton

All things are possible if you believe. I trust you Jesus in where you are taking me. We walk by faith and not by sight. Keep my mind stayed on thee.

L.E.A.R.N.   L.O.V.E.   L.E.A.D

DAY #100

1 PETER 4:8

NEW INTERNATIONAL VERSION

[8] Above all, love each other deeply, because love covers over a multitude of sins.

PRAYER by Angela

****

Father I thank you for a humbling spirit because I haven't always been humble. Thank you for opening my eyes and ears. Father your word tells us that even thou we can see in the natural we are blind to the spirit. Father open my eyes in the spirit that I may see pass the flesh in Jesus' name.

AFFIRMATION

Marcia Harton

Teach me how and what to pray dear Lord. Help me to forgive others and myself when we mess up. Show me the way to be pleasing in your sight.

ROMANS 12:9-10

NEW INTERNATIONAL VERSION

[9] Love must be sincere. Hate what is evil; cling to what is good. [10] Be devoted to one another in love. Honor one another above yourselves.

PRAYER by Angela

****

Father I thank you for it is already done. No weapon form will ever prosper. Every tongue that tries to rise will be cut at its root from the start. We are victorious and we want be moved. We are stand on every word the preceded out the mouth of GOD... Today I give thanks to the creator for allowing us another opportunity to impact someone's LIFE. Father thank you in Jesus name amen amen amen.

AFFIRMATION

Betty J Lewis

Prayer is actions.

Ask and is shall be given. Seek and you shall find. And when you knock, It shall open .

So, believe It and CLAIM IT, IT'S YOURS!

L.E.A.R.N.   L.O.V.E.   L.E.A.D

DAY #102

ROMANS 13:10

NEW INTERNATIONAL VERSION

[10] Love does no harm to a neighbor. Therefore love is the
fulfillment of the law

PRAYER by Angela

**Father complete a good thang in me. Father I give you praise
on today. I lift you up on this day because your word
reminds me that Love is action, Love is kind, Love is meek,
Love is patience, Love is obedience and LOVE covers.
Father I thank you for FAVOR in your son JESUS name.
Thank you for ACTIVATION right now
RESET<RENEW><RESTORE bah bah in Jesus name
AMEN .**

■■

AFFIRMATION

Allie West, Author, Speaker, Spiritual Healer

I AM THAT I AM

What ever I say I AM , I become.

When I say I AM, I summon the
attention of the Creator

I speak life, my I AM statements
represent what I wish to become

I am a Queen, a beautiful Masterpiece!

114

L.E.A.R.N.   L.O.V.E.   L.E.A.D

DAY #103

MARK 12:31

NEW INTERNATIONAL VERSION

[31] The second is this: 'Love your neighbor as yourself.'[a] There is no commandment greater than these.

PRAYER by Angela

****

Father

YOUR WILL FOR MY LIFE

I AM POWERLESS ONLY THRU YOU I HAVE POWER REMOVE ME OUT OF THE WAY.

IN JESUS NAME I PRAY! AMEN

■■

AFFIRMATION

Shelly Knox

Depression is real and pain is severe, whatever it is just give it to God and he'll see you through.

I had to learn to love me, I'm needed here.

DAY # 104

1 PETER 5:6-7

NEW INTERNATIONAL VERSION

[6] Humble yourselves, therefore, under God's mighty hand, that he may lift you up in due time. [7] Cast all your anxiety on him because he cares for you.

PRAYER by Angela

****

Father I thank you because you will hide us in present sight to be seen when it our time to be seen for YOUR GLORY FATHER! Lord, I thank you for reminding me that your time is always the right time and it's always on time. No matter what it looks like in the physical you are always working in the spirit on our behalf. Father I give you praise because you are truly worthy in Jesus name amen.

AFFIRMATION

Diana Hill

You are like a sunrise you shine in every condition. Adjust like the Sunrise still you shine through the clouds even in bad climate. Always shine no matter what

DAY #105

PROVERBS 3:3-4

NEW INTERNATIONAL VERSION

[3] Let love and faithfulness never leave you;
bind them around your neck,
write them on the tablet of your heart.
[4] Then you will win favor and a good name
in the sight of God and man.

PRAYER by Angela

****

**Father allow my fruit to speak for me. Father never allow
me to boast or brag. Keep me humble and stayed on your
word. All that you promised me shall come to manifestation
in my life in Jesus' name amen.**

AFFIRMATION

Sheela Wiley

Looked in the mirror and who did I see? I saw God's masterpiece staring back at me. Dress yourself up, get out and conquer the world.

DAY #106

Luke 6:31

New International Version

³¹ Do to others as you would have them do to you.

PRAYER by Angela

****

Not my will but your will. Today father I pray for those that despitefully use me. NO weapon formed against me will ever prosper. The POWER of the living God is in me, his blood runs thru me and I am all he said I am… I want be moved in Jesus name. Amen

■■

AFFIRMATION

Keywana Wright Jones

I will not be defeated.

For I am with thee, saith the Lord, to deliver you. Jeremiah 1:19

Dear God, thank you for fighting for me. I am victorious.

L.E.A.R.N.   L.O.V.E.   L.E.A.D

DAY # 107

PROVERBS 3:3-4

NEW INTERNATIONAL VERSION

[3] Let love and faithfulness never leave you;
bind them around your neck,
write them on the tablet of your heart.
[4] Then you will win favor and a good name
in the sight of God and man

PRAYER by Angela

****

FATHER GOD

I THANK YOU FOR FAVOR

IN JESUS NAME,

YOUR WILL NOT MINES

AFFIRMATION

Keywana Wright Jones
I except to receive a blessing.

Give and it shall be given to
you. Luke 6:38

Dear God, thank you for
blessing me when I give.
Amen

L.E.A.R.N.   L.O.V.E.   L.E.A.D

DAY #108

PSALM 86:15

NEW INTERNATIONAL VERSION

[15] But you, Lord, are a compassionate and gracious God, slow to anger, abounding in love and faithfulness.

PRAYER by Angela

****

Father God, I thank you for the opportunity to come before your throne to petition the heavens on behalf of my sisters and brothers. Father allow your spirit to fall a fresh on us today, allow our lives to be a living example of your LOVE. This is my prayer in Jesus name.

AFFIRMATION

Pastor Leah Legrone

Let's reflect on God's Grace today. His Amazing Grace that will empower you to learn, love, and lead. Trust that it is enough! It's made perfect in your weakness. 2 Corinthians 12:9.

L.E.A.R.N.   L.O.V.E.   L.E.A.D

DAY #109

1 JOHN 4:12

NEW INTERNATIONAL VERSION

[12] No one has ever seen God; but if we love one another, God
lives in us and his love is made complete in us

PRAYER by Angela

****

**Father I am constantly reminded of Genesis 2:7 where it
says you breathed the breath of LIFE in me so a piece of
you will always be with me. I can never be without you so
every time I look in the mirror, I see you. Father thanks
for revealing your truth to me. Father I thank you that
LOVE draws, LOVE covers a multitude of sin. Thank you
for loving me in Jesus' name.**

■■■

AFFIRMATION

Stephanie Johnson-Rice

You are so dope! Dope
gets you high; makes you
believe you can do
anything, alters perception;
you do what others don't
do to get it! Show the world
YOU!

121

DAY # 110

JOHN 13:34

NEW INTERNATIONAL VERSION

[34] "A new command I give you: Love one another. As I have loved you, so you must love one another.

PRAYER by Annette Martin

****

Our father who art in heaven thank you for watching over me & my family. Please forgive me for my sins known and unknown, thank you father for blessing me & my family.

■■■

AFFIRMATION

Minister Carrie L. Thomas

I know who I am. I am a capable and intelligent virtuous woman of God. God took His time to fearfully and wonderfully make me in His own image.

L.E.A.R.N.   L.O.V.E.   L.E.A.D

DAY #111

LEVITICUS 19:18

NEW INTERNATIONAL VERSION

18 "'Do not seek revenge or bear a grudge against anyone among your people, but love your neighbor as yourself. I am the LORD.

PRAYER by Annette Martin

****

Heavenly Father thank you for waking me up this day, starting me on my way clothed in my right mind. Amen.

■■ı

AFFIRMATION

Pastor J. SeNay Spurgeon

"The Lord, Our GOD Has PrOMiSed To Keep US!!! THE PuPoSe for Him Keeping US Once Is So That WE Will Have A Point of Reference of His Keeping POWER WhenEver We NEED to Be Kept AGAIN!!!

OFTEN, Our Dilemma is That WE Keep Forgetting GODS' ProMiSes To US!!!

So When Life Presents US With AFFLICTIONS, PreSent OUR AFFLICTIONS To OUR Keeper!!! God is A GOD That Can Do ANYTHING But Fail!!!

ToDay: Thank GOD for Keeping YOU By OwNing And HONORING How He Has ALREADY Kept You!!! Glory!!!"

L.E.A.R.N.   L.O.V.E.   L.E.A.D

DAY #112

PROVERBS 17:17

NEW INTERNATIONAL VERSION

[17] A friend loves at all times,
and a brother is born for a time of adversity.

PRAYER by Annette Martin
■■■

**Good morning Jesus thank you for a new day you have given
me, please help me to focus on what's right, help me to
change what I can and to leave the rest in your hands. In
Jesus name I pray.**

■■■

AFFIRMATION

Tajika Giles

Don't wait until you
have reached your
goals to be proud of
who you are. Be
proud of yourself for
taking the necessary
steps to achieve your
goals for better
opportunities in the
future.

DAY # 113

MATTHEW 22:37

NEW INTERNATIONAL VERSION

[37] Jesus replied: "'Love the Lord your God with all your heart and with all your soul and with all your mind.'

PRAYER by Annette Martin

****

Our father as I lay down to sleep, please relax my mind, body and soul. Help me to rest in you. I cast all my cares upon you, so that when I rise fresh and anew the next morning in Jesus. His words say weeping may endure for a night but JOY cometh in the morning. In Jesus name peace shall be mines. Amen.

AFFIRMATION

Constance Mckinsey Neal

You may feel it's not worth the hassle, the stress, the fight or the struggle.

God has a plan for your life. Trust his process regardless of what you see.

DAY #114

ROMANS 13:8

NEW INTERNATIONAL VERSION

[8] Let no debt remain outstanding, except the continuing debt to love one another, for whoever loves others has fulfilled the law.

PRAYER by Annette Martin

****

Lord God give peace to all those that are going thru troubled times right now in their lives. Father we are crying out asking for healing all over the land from all diseases that have come upon us. Lord you said if we ask you will deliver, Lord please heal us in Jesus' name Amen. And it is so in Jesus' name.

■■

AFFIRMATION

Kenya Reid

Keep pushing forward in spite of any life challenges keep pushing and leaning on God he will carry you through.

DAY #115

PSALM 143:8

NEW INTERNATIONAL VERSION

[8] Let the morning bring me word of your unfailing love,
for I have put my trust in you.
Show me the way I should go,
for to you I entrust my life.

PRAYER By Annette Martin

■■

Father your will not mines

**Father I speak healing all over this land. Father every trap
for the enemy set for my family and those attached to me I
call it cancelled right now. Sickness and diseases have no
place in my journey, and I rebuke that hinderance spirit
right now. Go back to the pits of hell. My word tells me I am
HEALED AND I WILL TRUST THE REPORT OF THE
LORD.**

AFFIRMATION

Tiffany S Hooks
Being rebuilt after you've
been broken is a beautiful
thing. Flourish through every
step of your journey. Lean
not on your own
understanding because you
will fail every time.

L.E.A.R.N.   L.O.V.E.   L.E.A.D

DAY # 116

GALATIANS 5:13

NEW INTERNATIONAL VERSION

[13] You, my brothers and sisters, were called to be free. But do not use your freedom to indulge the flesh[a]; rather, serve one another humbly in love.

PRAYER by Annette Martin

****

Thank you, Lord, for a new day, thank you for a roof over my head, clothes on my back, shoes on my feet. Father thank you for a car to drive, food to eat a job to labor on. Lord thank you for freedom to be able to enjoy LIFE and those on this journey with me. Father I thank you right now for Favor with you and Man. Amen Amen

■■

AFFIRMATION

Tiffany S Hooks

I will embrace my challenge and welcome the changes coming forth. There will be obstacles before us and we cannot allow them to sidetrack us. Remain on the path you are on and get the strength from with you make it through roadblocks

128

1 THESSALONIANS 3:12

NEW INTERNATIONAL VERSION

[12] May the Lord make your love increase and overflow for each other and for everyone else, just as ours does for you

PRAYER by Annette Martin

****

Father I pray that you will keep watch over us in our going in and out. Father no hurt harm or danger come nah us. Father shield and protect us from the crown of our head to the soles of our feet. Father your will be done thru us on this day. Let it not be about us Father but to bring you Glory. You are worthy of all our praise and if you don't do another thang, you have already done enough. I am here.

■■■

AFFIRMATION

Author Michelle Cain

Step out on Faith. Living in FEAR can LIMIT how far you will go in life but on the other side of fear awaits blessings and greatness for you.

129

DAY #118

1 JOHN 4:19

NEW INTERNATIONAL VERSION

[19] We love because he first loved us.

PRAYER by Annette Martin

****

Father I humble myself today to be used by You, Your will for my life not mine. I am just a willing vessel to be used for your glory. Allow your LOVE to shine thru me today in JESUS name AMEN.

■■■

AFFIRMATION

Mary Kennedy

Love. RePent. Seek.
Knock. Ask. Fast. Pray.
Believe In Mind/Heart
Confess w/Mouth. Know,
For YourSelf. Study. Hear.
Do, IN Obedience. Go.
Teach. Baptize.
ReMember. FearNOT.
Press. Be You!
#RockTrue^

1 CORINTHIANS 13:13

NEW INTERNATIONAL VERSION

[13] And now these three remain: faith, hope and love. But the greatest of these is love.

PRAYER by Annette Martin

****

Father when I can't do anything else I will believe in FAITH, stand in HOPE and LOVE unconditional because In you I know all things are possible and The only hope I have is in your word and truth Father you complete the great work you started in me. I'll be sure to give you all the praise and glory. In Jesus name I pray.

■■

AFFIRMATION

13

Rolanda T. Pyle

It's all about perspective - Others said Goliath was too big to hit. David said he was too big to miss. Go for it!

L.E.A.R.N. L.O.V.E. L.E.A.D

DAY #120

JOHN 15:13

NEW INTERNATIONAL VERSION

[13] Greater love has no one than this: to lay down one's life for one's friends.

PRAYER by Annette Martin

■■■

Dear God, thank you for waking me up this day, thanking you for bringing me thru changes in my body and complete healing. Father your word said by Jesus stripes we are healed. So today I speak healing over everyone that reads this today. Whatever ailment trying to attach to your body will not manifest it will be stopped in its track. I speak complete healing right now in JESUS name amen.

■■

AFFIRMATION

Leesa Michelle

let me go so I can grow. Did I mention I'm the CEO? intelligence is relevant so get a clue and watch it brew.

132

L.E.A.R.N.   L.O.V.E.   L.E.A.D

DAY #121

PROVERBS 2:6-8

NEW INTERNATIONAL VERSION

⁶ For the LORD gives wisdom;
from his mouth come knowledge and understanding.
⁷ He holds success in store for the upright,
he is a shield to those whose walk is blameless,
⁸ for he guards the course of the just
and protects the way of his faithful ones.

PRAYER by Angela

**Father today my pray is that you have heard our prayers
over the last 121 days and you have answered them
according to your will for our LIVES. Father we wanted be
moved by what we see in the natural we will stand on your
word until it is perfected in our lives. In Jesus Name amen.**

■■■

AFFIRMATION

Stephanie Johnson-Rice

Authenticity is key. If you are not your genuine self, then you are robbing the world of the brilliance lying within you. Exhibit that righteous radiance! Go forth--be great!

L.E.A.R.N.   L.O.V.E.   L.E.A.D

LOVE

L- Looking pass our flesh and seeing the Jesus in us.

O- Overcomer, despite all that came at me I am still standing.

V -Value know your worth and understanding you are more precious than Diamonds and as rare as GEM

E- Evolve, willing to grow in the things of God to ensure Enteral Life.

Author Pamela J Hayes

The original brown girl loves to create a world on paper to make people think, teach kids self-love

DAY # 1

Deuteronomy 4:27

King James Version

27 And the Lord shall scatter you among the nations, and ye shall be left few in number among the heathen, whither the Lord shall lead you.

PRAYER

Thank you, father, for waking up us this morning. Thank. You for covering me, my family, my sisters in Christ. I pray for love for everyone. God teach them and show them how to love themselves. If they cannot love themselves, how are they going to love one another. These and all blessings we ask in Jesus' name Amen.

****

AFFIRMATION

Leesa Michelle
Because Gods not finished he replenishes and relinquishes his love like a dove smiling above cause I know I'm

loved   ☐ Stay
Blessed

DAY #2

Judges 5:12

New International Version

[12] 'Wake up, wake up, Deborah!
Wake up, wake up, break out in song!
Arise, Barak!
Take captive your captives, son of Abinoam.'

PRAYER

Father in the name of Jesus. God is love. Love is God. God, please teach us how to love unconditionally. Show us how to love no matter what the situation is. Love doesn't care what you did, what you said, what happen, you need to just love the person no matter what. I love you! Sister, God loves you first. In Jesus name Amen.

****

AFFIRMATION

Nichole Henderson

The inside of you once you deal with your issues. A lot of times in life we choose to deal with the surface of a matter, however it takes getting to the root of an issue in order for true change to take place in our lives.

L.E.A.R.N.   L.O.V.E.   L.E.A.D

DAY #3

Psalm 5:8

New International Version

[8] Lead me, LORD, in your righteousness
because of my enemies—
make your way straight before me.

PRAYER

****

Father God in the name of Jesus, we need to show love to the
world in. these trying times. God show us how to be strong and
love each with this COVID VIRSUS. Show how to love with no
fear. If we know you God, we should have no fear. God be with
us, teach us how to love through the fear in Jesus' name. Amen.
****

AFFIRMATION

Author

Eleanor R. Tye

Learn = As I learn about my
journey of life, I find myself
reminiscing about the
profound advice that my
wise elders had passed on
to me and I gladly share my
indispensable experiences
with eager listeners...

139

DAY # 4

Psalm 25:5

New International Version

⁵ Guide me in your truth and teach me,
for you are God my Savior,
and my hope is in you all day long

PRAYER

****

Father God in the name of Jesus Love is an action word Lord.
So please teach us how to show love. Allow us to show how love
feels, how we can show love, teach us Lord how to also receive
love. In Jesus name we pray amen.

AFFIRMATION

Author

Eleanor R. Tye

Love = I love the Lord
Jesus Christ
because he first
loved me. He has
taught me how to
love myself and
others.

L.E.A.R.N.   L.O.V.E.   L.E.A.D

DAY #5

Psalm 27:11

New International Version

¹¹ Teach me your way, LORD;
lead me in a straight path
because of my oppressors.

.'

PRAYER

****

Father God, in the name of Jesus, teach us how to accept love.
Let us know we are worthy to be loved. Jesus shows us how to
receive your love in Jesus' name amen

****

AFFIRMATION

Author Eleanor R. Tye

Lead = When I am asked to take the lead at the food pantry that I currently volunteer at, I keep the rules and merits in mind along with a few of my significant recommendations

DAY #6

Psalm 31:3

New International Version

³ Since you are my rock and my fortress,
for the sake of your name lead and guide me..

PRAYER

****

Father God in the name of Jesus teach us how to love through the pain. The pain of hurt from our fellow man. How to love through the pain of illness. How to love through the pain of death. Show us how to love in all situations. Show us and teach us that love is the most powerful feeling that can heal all in Jesus' name we pray Amen.

****

AFFIRMATION

Chinyelu Uduchukwu-Akpaka
To learn is to journey to the world of the unknown
To learn is to be alive
To learn is to be a better you
It pays to learn

142

L.E.A.R.N.   L.O.V.E.   L.E.A.D

DAY # 7

Psalm 43:3

New International Version

³ Send me your light and your faithful care,
let them lead me;
let them bring me to your holy mountain,
to the place where you dwell.

PRAYER

****

Father God in the name of Jesus teach us how to love you lord. Teach us how to show you love by being obedient. By listening to you lord with our spiritual ear. By reading our bible lord by getting to know you Lord. By turning every situation over to you lord and wait. Wait for you Jesus. Teach us that love is being obedient to your word in Jesus' name. Amen.
****

AFFIRMATION

Char Prince

Lord we are asking for your love to shower us today. Speak to our hearts and minds, let us know that we do matter and we are loved by you..

DAY #8

Psalm 61:2

New International Version

² From the ends of the earth I call to you,
I call as my heart grows faint;
lead me to the rock that is higher than I.

PRAYER

****

Father God in the name of Jesus, love is a healing. Jesus Show us how love shows up with healing power. Take love to the hospital rooms, the hospital halls, touch the doctors, the nurses, the housekeepers, everyone in the hospital and touch with your love Jesus. Love is healing. Go in the hospitals and heal, and bring people home to their loved ones. Show them the healing power of love in Jesus' name Amen

****

AFFIRMATION

R.C. Nichole

I am made in my Father's image. Fearfully and wonderfully made. Unapologetically bold. I embrace my peculiarities. God has set me apart; my destiny is unique for building his Kingdom. (Psalm 139:14)

DAY #9

Psalm 143:10

New International Version

[10] Teach me to do your will,
for you are my God;
may your good Spirit
lead me on level ground.

PRAYER

****

Father God in the name of Jesus. Help me lord with depression. Lord I need your love so much today I am suffering with a depression spirit. But I know that the God I serve is a mighty God and if he loves me this depression spirit has to flee. Love heals all. Thank you, Jesus, for your love, Love from my God pushes out anything that is not of him. So, depression must flee, hurt, must flee, being afraid must flee, thank you Jesus for showing me your love. In Jesus name amen.

****

AFFIRMATION

JAZZMIN RAINE

"The best that you can give others , is by loving you first "

DAY # 10

Proverbs 8:20

New International Version

[20] I walk in the way of righteousness,
along the paths of justice

PRAYER

****

Father god in the name of Jesus Lord teach me how to love when someone has hurt me. Teach me how to love when everything is going wrong. Teach me how to love everyone no matter what is going on. Jesus' name we pray amen.

****

AFFIRMATION

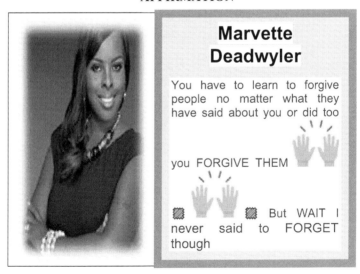

Marvette Deadwyler

You have to learn to forgive people no matter what they have said about you or did too

you FORGIVE THEM

But WAIT I never said to FORGET though

L.E.A.R.N.   L.O.V.E.   L.E.A.D

DAY #11

Proverbs 6:22

New International Version

[22] When you walk, they will guide you;
when you sleep, they will watch over you;
when you awake, they will speak to you.

PRAYER

****

Father God in the name of Jesus Lord Teach me how to love
people behind the bars. Show me how to love them with faults.
Show me how to love by not judging. Show me how to love all
God's Children no matter what they have done. No matter what
is going on in their lives I need to love people where they are at
in their lives. Lord show me in Jesus' name Amen.
****

AFFIRMATION

Sheena Gee

I'm going to Lead
with love in my
heart. I won't let
hate, tension, anger,
jealousy and rage in
my heart instead
I'll let Peace become
me.

L.E.A.R.N.   L.O.V.E.   L.E.A.D

DAY #12

Isaiah 42:16

New International Version

[16] I will lead the blind by ways they have not known,
along unfamiliar paths I will guide them;
I will turn the darkness into light before them
and make the rough places smooth.
These are the things I will do;
I will not forsake them.

PRAYER

****

Father God in the name of Jesus please teach me self-love. Teach me to love me in my own skin. Teach me how to look at myself from head to toe and love what I see, teach me how to embrace myself and love me from inside out in Jesus' name we pray amen.
****

AFFIRMATION

Mechell Davis
Love
LOVE is more than just a four letter word. LOVE is not just something you tell someone. Let the Most High bring you unfailing and genuine LOVE, because action behind the word LOVE is what make it efficient and meaningful.

148

L.E.A.R.N.   L.O.V.E.   L.E.A.D

DAY # 13

Isaiah 57:18

New International Version

[18] I have seen their ways, but I will heal them;
I will guide them and restore comfort to Israel's mourners,

PRAYER

****

Father God please help me love my inner self. Teach me to love my mind, my dreams, love my goals, love everything and anything about Pamela. In Jesus name I pray amen.

****

AFFIRMATION

Chinchila Jonesia

'I AM' *Beautiful*... 'I AM' *Kind*...

'I AM' *Loving*...'I AM' *Lovable*...

'I AM' *Loved*...'I AM' *Unique*...

"I AM A CHILD OF THE MOST HIGH"

"I AM" ..... *Chinchila Jonesia!!!*

DAY #14

Luke 6:39

New International Version

[39] He also told them this parable: "Can the blind lead the blind? Will they not both fall into a pit?

PRAYER

✶✶

Father God in the name of Jesus Thank you for teaching me how to love myself. Jesus thank you for teaching me self-love which we need to know how to do. In Jesus name Amen.

✶✶

AFFIRMATION

REV, ESSIES DAVIS
LEAD
Take time initiative to be an effective leader. Lead is to show someone the way to go by moving forward in whatever direction they desire to go in their life.

L.E.A.R.N.   L.O.V.E.   L.E.A.D

DAY #15

Matthew 15:14

New International Version

14 Leave them; they are blind guides.[a] If the blind lead the blind, both will fall into a pit."

PRAYER

****

Father God in the name of Jesus thank you for the love of our site. We take that for granted but I thank you for how I can see. With my eyes. With my spiritual eyes, and my vision. Thank you for allowing me to see the beauty of the trees, the flowers, the birds, all the scenery that Jesus that you create for us to see. Thank you, lord, in Jesus' name I pray amen.

****

AFFIRMATION

REV ESSIE DAVIS (LEAD)

. We want others to see what God has done in our life and they will say "If God can do it for her or him he can do it for me" I will follow after her lead. Be a role model for others to follow you because they respect and admire you.

151

DAY # 16

Matthew 6:13

New International Version

[13] And lead us not into temptation,[a]
but deliver us from the evil one.[b]'

PRAYER

****

Father God in the name of Jesus for the love of taste. Thank you for allowing us to taste all the amazing foods, candies, you allow us to taste and experience. Thank you for the power of our tongue for taste and to talk. In Jesus name amen.

AFFIRMATION

Deborah A. Franklin

I will live my life out loud because that is what I was created to do as I walk in my purpose on my way to my destiny!

DAY #17

Revelation 7:17

New International Version

[17] For the Lamb at the center of the throne
will be their shepherd;
'he will lead them to springs of living water.'[a]
'And God will wipe away every tear from their eyes.'

PRAYER

****

Father God in the name of Jesus thank you for allowing me the scent of touch. Thank you for the power of the touch. Thank you for allowing us to have hands, arms, fingers. I love how we can feel different textures, how we can feed ourselves, take care of ourselves, by taking a bath, cooking, cleaning, feeling each other, the power of touch is amazing. Thank you, Lord in Jesus name Amen.

****

AFFIRMATION

Nicho Charisse
You are a unique soul as it should be. God creates you in His image. Continue to grow with the spirit and power that manifest within you. Uniquely

DAY #18

Psalm 23:3

New International Version

³ he refreshes my soul.
He guides me along the right paths
for his name's sake.

PRAYER

****

Father God thank you for the love of the use of my legs & feet.
Thank you for the power of walking and feeling with my feet.
Thank you for allowing me to walk and the use of my legs, and
feet. Thank you for allowing me the power of walking. How
we can swim, and be in the water and on land. In Jesus name I
pray Amen.

AFFIRMATION

Lisa Renee Halliburton

We need to look beyond our
faults just like our Father
does in heaven. Forgive
yourself and release it from
your heart and soul.

Push Forward, believe in
yourself, and know your
worth! That inner strength
and feeling are real, so act on
it with haste! Move in love
and grace

God makes all things
Possible.

DAY # 19

Jeremiah 29:13

New International Version

[13] You will seek me and find me when you seek me with all your heart.

PRAYER

****

Father God in the name of Jesus thank for the love of sound with my ears. Thank you, lord, for allowing me to hear the sound of your voice. Thank you for allowing me to hear the sounds you have created in the world. Thank you for the sound of all animals, the sound of nature. I love to just listen to the beautiful music you make with thunder, and rain fall. That is a blessing. Thank you, Jesus, in your name I pray amen.

AFFIRMATION

Minister Margaret Parker

LOVE

Love is a very important part of life. In order to succeed in anything we have to first get GOD involved in it, we also have to have a passion for whatever we are doing

155

DAY #20

Galatians 6:9

New International Version

[9] Let us not become weary in doing good, for at the proper time we will reap a harvest if we do not give up.

PRAYER

****

Father God in the name of Jesus thank you for the love of smell. My nose. Thank you for allowing me to be able to smell the millions of scents in the world. Thank you in Jesus' name Amen.

****

AFFIRMATION

Author
Zipporah Israel

. I am a being of love
I am happy.
I am magnificent.
I am a powerful
manifester.
I create the life I
want.

L.E.A.R.N.   L.O.V.E.   L.E.A.D

DAY #21

Philippians 2:3

New International Version

[3] Do nothing out of selfish ambition or vain conceit. Rather, in humility value others above yourselves,

PRAYER

****

Father God thank you for the love of my sisters that re praying with me on this journey. Thank you for the love that Angela gives unconditionally. Thank you for giving her this assignment and she sharing the love with me. Thank you for allowing us to grow stronger in this prayer journey. In Jesus name I pray amen.

AFFIRMATION

PAMELA EDWARDS
INTIMACY ♥
I AM ALONE BUT NOT LONELY
I AM A OFFERING BUT NOT
OFFENDED
I AM VICTORIOUS BUT NOT A VICTIM
I AM EVERLASTING BUT NOT
ENVIOUS
I AM LOVE, INTIMACY (INTO ME SEE)
LOVE ALWAYS

DAY # 22

Philippians 4:13

New International Version

[13] I can do all this through him who gives me strength.

PRAYER

****

Father God thank you for the love of having a husband for the third time. But this love Jesus I know its correct because you were in the mist from start to now. The way we met, the way we read the one-year holy bible together, the way the day of our wedding you gave me a sign on the Saturday, January 11,2020 the weather was 70 degrees which was the sign you gave me to let me know yes, I was supposed to marry him. Thank you, lord, for giving me a life partner to love me, to protect me, to be my best friend, for me to teacher him the love of the lord. Thank you, lord, in Jesus' name Amen.

AFFIRMATION

Auset Atun Re

Aum' Let Us Meditate On That Excellent Glory Of The Divine Light. May They Stimulate Our Understandings.

L.E.A.R.N.   L.O.V.E.   L.E.A.D

DAY #23

Proverbs 27:23

New International Version

²³ Be sure you know the condition of your flocks,
give careful attention to your herds;

PRAYER

****

Father God in the name of Jesus thank you for the love of my parents. They taught me unconditional love first. They taught me the love of family. Thank you for showing me how to love my family unconditionally in Jesus' name Amen.

****

AFFIRMATION

Chaka Davis Smith

Learning is a part of life. It is an ongoing LESSON you pursue everyday. With every obstacle, trial, tribulation we face, with GOD'S help we will always learn that there is triumph, a message, a success in store for us. KEEP growing, KEEP learning , Learn something new today.

DAY #24

Luke 6:31

New International Version

[31] Do to others as you would have them do to you.

PRAYER

****

Father God in the name Jesus thank you for the love of friendship. Friendships become your family that love of friendship is pure, its amazing, it grows. 2:02 PM Thank you Jesus for the love of friendship on Jesus' name Amen.

****

AFFIRMATION

Monica Reese aka MonRee

Praying for you and with you. Everyday is a good day for you, you must speak it into existence. Our words have power, speak life over this and all other situations. I love you to life sis!!! You've got this!!! You can do all things through CHRIST JESUS!!!.

DAY # 25

Matthew 20:26

New International Version

[26] Not so with you. Instead, whoever wants to become great among you must be your servant,

PRAYER

****

Father God in the name of Jesus thank you for the love of sisterhood. Sisters can be by blood or you find each other by choice. Sisterly love is beautiful and needed. Thank you for the love of sisterhood Amen.

AFFIRMATION

Monica Reese aka MonRee

Applying pressure to a wound stops the bleeding. This pressure that you feel is stopping a wound from bleeding out and saving lives in the process!!! No weapon formed against you shall ever prosper!!! I love you to life!!!

Proverbs 29:11

New International Version

[11] Fools give full vent to their rage,
but the wise bring calm in the end

,

PRAYER

****

Father God in the name of Jesus thank you for showing the love
of a church family. That is some powerful love. Praying love,
healing love, community love. Thank you love for church love
in Jesus' name. Amen.

AFFIRMATION

Dominique E
Jones

If it doesn't get
better,

you get better.

DAY #27

Luke 22:26

New International Version

²⁶ But you are not to be like that. Instead, the greatest among you should be like the youngest, and the one who rules like the one who serve.

PRAYER

****

Father God in the name of Jesus Lord thank you for the love of myself. Thank you for teaching me how to love myself. Thank you for teaching me how to love everything about myself. If I don't know how to love me Jesus how can I love others. Thank you for self-love in Jesus' name Amen.

****

AFFIRMATION

Dominique E Jones

Dare to thank God even it doesn't make sense

DAY # 28

Matthew 20:26

New International Version

²⁶ Not so with you. Instead, whoever wants to become great among you must be your servant,

PRAYER

****

Father God in the name of Jesus thank you Lord for showing me how to love mankind. Showing me how to humble myself. Thank you for showing how to love everyone how you love us unconditional. Everyone you have taught me need love. Thank you, Jesus, in your name Amen.

****

AFFIRMATION

Dominique E Jones

People know your worth. They just hope you don't

DAY #29

Mark 9:35

New International Version

[35] Sitting down, Jesus called the Twelve and said, "Anyone who wants to be first must be the very last, and the servant of all."

PRAYER

****

Father God in the name of Jesus' lord love is a powerful word. Love is an action word. Jesus, you taught me that its not just saying the words, you must put action behind it. Thank you, Jesus. In your name Jesus, I love you Lord the way you never turn your back on me. I love you Jesus for always by my side. Jesus thank you for loving me by my side every step even when I didn't know you Jesus. Thank you in Jesus' name I pray Amen.

****

AFFIRMATION

Dominique E Jones

If you don't rest your soul in Jesus, you'll never find peace and purpose

DAY #30

Hebrews 13:7

New International Version

[7] Remember your leaders, who spoke the word of God to you. Consider the outcome of their way of life and imitate their faith.

PRAYER

****

Father God in the name of Jesus. Love Jesus thank you for allowing me to find Love. Thank you for allowing me to feel love. Thank you, Jesus, for teaching me how to love in Jesus' name Amen.

AFFIRMATION

Queen
Angela

LOVE IS
FREE

DAY # 31

Romans 1:1

New International Version

1 Paul, a servant of Christ Jesus, called to be an apostle and set apart for the gospel of God—

PRAYER

****

Father God in the name of Jesus thank you for showing me the love of creativity. Thank you for giving the love of being able to imagine beautiful worlds and dreams, translate it to paper and share it to the world. Thank you for allowing me to become an author. I love to write and you taught me how to love my craft. In Jesus name amen.

****

AFFIRMATION

DAY #32

Matthew 20:28

New International Version

28 just as the Son of Man did not come to be served, but to serve, and to give his life as a ransom for many."

PRAYER

****

Father God in the name of Jesus God is love.   Love is God. Thank you for your love thank you for never leaving my side. Thank you, Lord. Just thank you for loving me. And teaching me that I am always going to be love by you no matter what thank you Lord. Jesus' name Amen.

****

AFFIRMATION

Queen Angela

LOVE IS KIND

L.E.A.R.N.   L.O.V.E.   L.E.A.D

DAY #33

1 Timothy 4:12

New International Version

[12] Don't let anyone look down on you because you are young, but set an example for the believers in speech, in conduct, in love, in faith and in purity..

PRAYER

****

Father God in the name of Jesus Thank you for showing us how to love animals. Thank you for the love of animals. They have healing power for a lot of people who are lonely. The love of an animals, help children learn how to take care love ones and responsibility. The love of animals is a beautiful thing. Thank you, Jesus, for showing so many ways to love in Jesus' name. Amen.

****

AFFIRMATION

Rolanda T Pyle

I will live and not die
I will speak truth and not lie
I am delivered, no longer bound
God has healed me, He's turned it around!

169

DAY # 34

2 Timothy 2:15

New International Version

[15] Do your best to present yourself to God as one approved, a worker who does not need to be ashamed and who correctly handles the word of truth.

PRAYER

****

Father God in the name of Jesus thank you for showing the love the church. The church is our family as well. Families are messy, they fight, they cry together, feel hope together, pray together and we will take care of our family. We take care of our own. Thank you, Jesus, for the love of the church. In Jesus name Amen

AFFIRMATION

Queen Angela
John 15:12: My command is this: Love each other as I have loved you.

DAY #35

Mark 10:45

New International Version

[45] For even the Son of Man did not come to be served, but to serve, and to give his life as a ransom for many."

PRAYER

****

Father God in the name of Jesus thank you for the love of family. Thank you teaching how to our family when we do not like them. Thank you for teaching us how to love our family when we are sad. Teaching us how to love our family when we are hurting. Thank you for teaching our family in times of sorrow. Thank you, Jesus, for the love of family in Jesus' name Amen.

AFFIRMATION

Queen Angela

Corinthians 16:14: Do everything in love

DAY #36

Isaiah 41:10

New International Version

[10] So do not fear, for I am with you;
do not be dismayed, for I am your God.
I will strengthen you and help you;
I will uphold you with my righteous right hand

PRAYER

****

Father God in the name of Jesus thank you for the love of Christ.
Thank you, Jesus, for loving me. Loving me with all my faults,
my mistakes, my pain, my faith not being as strong as it should
be, thank you Jesus for always loving me in Jesus' name I pray
Amen.

AFFIRMATION

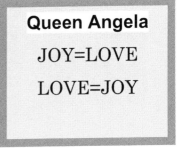

Queen Angela

JOY=LOVE

LOVE=JOY

DAY # 37

John 3:30

New International Version

[30] He must become greater; I must become less.

PRAYER

****

Father God in the name of Jesus thank you for the love of friends. I thank you for placing people in my life that will love me and remove people that I believed that loved me and was doing right by me. Thank you, Jesus, for loving me in all these situations. In Jesus name we pray Amen

****

AFFIRMATION

Queen Angela

L-LEARNED

O-OBSERVED

V-VULNERABLE

E-ENGAGING.

DAY #38

Matthew 7:12

New International Version

[12] So in everything, do to others what you would have them do to you, for this sums up the Law and the Prophets.

PRAYER

****

Father God in the name of Jesus thank you for showing me how to love myself. Thank you Jesus for teaching me the importance of self-love. Thank you for teaching me to love myself and to put my heart first. Thank you Jesus in your sons name Amen.

****

AFFIRMATION

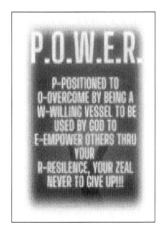

DAY #39

Proverbs 4:23

New International Version

²³ Above all else, guard your heart,
for everything you do flows from it.

PRAYER

****

Father God in the name of Jesus thank you lord for the love of my children. Thank you for allowing me to be a parent. Thank you for allowing me to be a parent and experiencing love from my children. These and all blessings I ask in. Jesus name Amen.

****

AFFIRMATION

Queen Angela
LOVE SPEAKS

DAY # 40

Proverbs 29:2

New International Version

² When the righteous thrive, the people rejoice;
when the wicked rule, the people groan.

PRAYER

****

Father God in the name. of Jesus thank you for teaching me how
to love once I was hurt. Thank you for teaching to trust love
with people again. Thank you, Jesus, for teaching me love after
my heart was shattered. Thank you in Jesus' name Amen.
****

AFFIRMATION

DAY #41

Acts 20:28

New International Version

[28] Keep watch over yourselves and all the flock of which the Holy Spirit has made you overseers. Be shepherds of the church of God,[a] which he bought with his own blood

PRAYER

****

Father God in the name of Jesus thank you for love. Love is a beautiful feeling. Your love is warm, comforting, healing, healthy. Jesus' love is the best love you can feel. Thank you for the power of your love in Jesus' name Amen.

****

AFFIRMATION

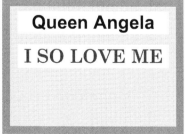

Queen Angela

I SO LOVE ME

DAY #42

Mark 9:42

New International Version

[42] "If anyone causes one of these little ones—those who believe in me—to stumble, it would be better for them if a large millstone were hung around their neck and they were thrown into the sea.

PRAYER

****

Father God in the name of Jesus thank you for the love of our parents. Thank you in Jesus' name amen.

****

AFFIRMATION

LaTonya Mullins

I affirm God's word that I will prosper in all things and be in good health, even as my soul prosper

John 3 1:2

DAY # 43

Psalm 124:2

New International Version

[2] if the LORD had not been on our side
when people attacked us,

PRAYER

****

Father God in the name of Jesus thank you Jesus for self-love.
Thank you for teaching us how to love ourselves. How to love
ourselves when we are sad when the world seems to be against
us. Thank you, Jesus, for self-love. In Jesus name Amen

****

AFFIRMATION

LaTonya Mullins
Before the foundations of the
earth God has already affirmed
us. Through God's divine
revelation, we have the power
to affirm ourself. Declaring
wholeness in all areas of our
lives.

DAY #44

Psalm 125:1

New International Version

[1] Those who trust in the LORD are like Mount Zion,
which cannot be shaken but endures forever.

PRAYER

****

Father God in the name of Jesus thank you for the love of your
siblings. Thank you for the love of your sisters, brothers, that
you choose and for your blood sisters, & brothers in Jesus' name
Amen.

AFFIRMATION

LaTonya Mullins

According to Corinthians 5:8
Christ is reconciled himself
to us and has given us the
ministry of reconciliation.

L.E.A.R.N.   L.O.V.E.   L.E.A.D

DAY #45

Psalm 127:1

New International Version

[1] Unless the LORD builds the house,
the builders labor in vain.
Unless the LORD watches over the city,
the guards stand watch in vain.

PRAYER

****

Father God in the name of Jesus thank you for the love strangers.
Thank you for teaching how to love perfect strangers. In Jesus
name amen.

****

AFFIRMATION

LaTonya Mullins

I declare healing and
restoration over our lives

L.E.A.R.N.   L.O.V.E.   L.E.A.D

DAY # 46

Psalm 122:1

New International Version

[1] I rejoiced with those who said to me,

"Let us go to the house of the LORD."

PRAYER

****

Father God in the name of Jesus thank you for the love of your

spouse. That is a special love. Thank you for the love for being

in love with your spouse and knowing this kind of love in Jesus'

name amen.

AFFIRMATION

Myra Starks

It's okay to help others, but don't help them so much that you can't help yourself. When we care for ourselves properly, we show others how to properly care for us.

DAY #47

Psalm 128:1

New International Version

[1] Blessed are all who fear the LORD,
who walk in obedience to him.

PRAYER

****

Father God in the name of Jesus thank you for the love of your
spouse. That is a special love. Thank you for the love for being
in love with your spouse and knowing this kind of love in Jesus'
name amen.

****

AFFIRMATION

ASHLEY
ABRAHAM

I AM
HUMBLED

DAY #48

Psalm 120:1

New International Version

[1] I call on the LORD in my distress,
and he answers me.

PRAYER

****

Father God in the name of Jesus thank you Jesus for loving me with all my imperfections. Thank you loving me when I am not praying and not being obedience to your word. Thank you in Jesus' name amen.

****

AFFIRMATION

ASHLEY ABRAHAM

I

AM

BLESSED

DAY #49

PSALM 134

NEW INTERNATIONAL VERSION

[1] Praise the LORD, all you servants of the LORD
who minister by night in the house of the LORD.
[2] Lift up your hands in the sanctuary
and praise the LORD.

[3] May the LORD bless you from Zion,
he who is the Maker of heaven and earth

PRAYER

****

Father God in the name of Jesus thank you for the love when we are back sliding. Thank you for the love when we are not praying, when we are in the world not reading the word, we are not tithing when we are not worshiping thank you for loving us in Jesus name amen.

AFFIRMATION

ASHLEY ABRAHAM

I

AM

LOVE

DAY #50

PSALM 130:1-2

NEW INTERNATIONAL VERSION

[1] Out of the depths I cry to you, LORD;
[2]   Lord, hear my voice.
    Let your ears be attentive
    to my cry for mercy.

PRAYER

****

Father God in the name of Jesus thank you for loving us When
we are not deserving of your love thank you in Jesus name
Amen.

■■

AFFIRMATION

Dominique E. Jones

The power of "no"
will save your
life...literally

DAY # 51

PROVERBS 1:5

NEW INTERNATIONAL VERSION

⁵ let the wise listen and add to their learning,
and let the discerning get guidance

PRAYER

****

Thank you, father, for waking up us this morning. Thank. You
for covering me, my family, my sisters in Christ. I pray for
love for everyone. God teach them and show them how to love
themselves. If they cannot love themselves, how are they
going to love one another. These and all blessings we ask in
Jesus' name Amen.

****

AFFIRMATION

Dominique E. Jones

People may not
understand but when you
need to shut down, DO
JUST THAT

187

DAY #52

PROVERBS 1:5

NEW INTERNATIONAL VERSION

⁵ let the wise listen and add to their learning,

and let the discerning get guidance

PRAYER

****

Father in the name of Jesus. God is love. Love is God. God,

please teach us how to love unconditionally. Show us how to

love no matter what the situation is. Love doesn't care what you

did, what you said, what happen, you need to just love the person

no matter what. I love you! Sister, God loves you first. In Jesus

name Amen

****

AFFIRMATION

Dominique E. Jones
It's ok if the only thing you do today is breathe.

L.E.A.R.N.   L.O.V.E.   L.E.A.D

DAY #53

PROVERBS 6:22

NEW INTERNATIONAL VERSION

²² When you walk, they will guide you;

when you sleep, they will watch over you;

when you awake, they will speak to you

PRAYER

****

Father God in the name of Jesus, we need to show love to the
world in. these trying times. God show us how to be strong and
love each with this COVID VIRSUS. Show how to love with no
fear. If we know you God, we should have no fear. God be with
us, teach us how to love through the fear in Jesus' name. Amen.

AFFIRMATION

Dominique E. Jones

There's no better
representation of strength
than someone who isn't
afraid of being
themselves...flaws
included

L.E.A.R.N.   L.O.V.E.   L.E.A.D

DAY # 54

PROVERBS 9:10

NEW INTERNATIONAL VERSION

[10] The fear of the LORD is the beginning of wisdom,
and knowledge of the Holy One is understanding.

PRAYER

****

Father God in the name of Jesus Love is an action word Lord.
So please teach us how to show love. Allow us to show how love
feels, how we can show love, teach us Lord how to also receive
love. In Jesus name we pray amen.

AFFIRMATION

Dominique E. Jones
People know your worth. They just hope you don't.

190

DAY #55

Proverbs 13:1

New International Version

13 A wise son heeds his father's instruction,
but a mocker does not respond to rebukes.'

PRAYER

****

Father God, in the name of Jesus, teach us how to accept love.
Let us know we are worthy to be loved. Jesus shows us how to
receive your love in Jesus' name amen.

****

AFFIRMATION

Dominique E. Jones

Promote
you...you're
somebody's answer

PROVERBS 16:3

NEW INTERNATIONAL VERSION

³ Commit to the LORD whatever you do,
and he will establish your plans.

PRAYER

****

Father God in the name of Jesus teach us how to love through the pain. The pain of hurt from our fellow man. How to love through the pain of illness. How to love through the pain of death. Show us how to love in all situations. Show us and teach us that love is the most powerful feeling that can heal all in Jesus' name we pray Amen.

****

AFFIRMATION

Dominique E. Jones

Your short term challenges aren't your long term no's.

DAY # 57

PROVERBS 18:21

NEW INTERNATIONAL VERSION

[21] The tongue has the power of life and death,
and those who love it will eat its fruit.

PRAYER

■■■I

Father God in the name of Jesus teach us how to love you lord.
Teach us how to show you love by being obedient. By listening
to you lord with our spiritual ear. By reading our bible lord by
getting to know you Lord. By turning every situation over to you
lord and wait. Wait for you Jesus. Teach us that love is being
obedient to your word in Jesus' name. Amen.

****

AFFIRMATION

Dominique E. Jones

The same ppl that said
you can't and you won't
are scared that you will
be

DAY #58

PROVERBS 20:11

NEW INTERNATIONAL VERSION

[11] Even small children are known by their actions,
so is their conduct really pure and upright?

PRAYER

****

.Father God in the name of Jesus, love is a healing. Jesus Show us how love shows up with healing power. Take love to the hospital rooms, the hospital halls, touch the doctors, the nurses, the housekeepers, everyone in the hospital and touch with your love Jesus. Love is healing. Go in the hospitals and heal, and bring people home to their loved ones. Show them the healing power of love in Jesus' name Amen.

****

AFFIRMATION

Dominique E. Jones

You should always be in a state of growing

L.E.A.R.N.   L.O.V.E.   L.E.A.D

DAY #59

PROVERBS 25:28

NEW INTERNATIONAL VERSION

²⁸ Like a city whose walls are broken through
is a person who lacks self-control.

PRAYER

****

.Father God in the name of Jesus. Help me lord with depression.
Lord I need your love so much today I am suffering with a
depression spirit. But I know that the God I serve is a mighty
God and as long as he loves me this depression spirit has to flee.
Love heals all. Thank you, Jesus, for your love, Love from my
God pushes out anything that is not of him. So, depression must
flee, hurt, must flee, being afraid must flee, thank you Jesus for
showing me your love. In Jesus name amen.

****

AFFIRMATION

Dominique E. Jones

You don't have to
root for me but at
least respect my
progress

195

L.E.A.R.N.   L.O.V.E.   L.E.A.D

DAY # 60

PROVERBS 27:1

NEW INTERNATIONAL VERSION

27 Do not boast about tomorrow,
for you do not know what a day may bring.

PRAYER

****

Father god in the name of Jesus Lord teach me how to love when someone has hurt me. Teach me how to love when everything is going wrong. Teach me how to love everyone no matter what is going on. Jesus' name we pray amen.

AFFIRMATION

Author Zipporah Israel
My mind is at peace
I am wealthy
I have a caring heart
I am great in everything I do
Everything always works out for me

L.E.A.R.N.   L.O.V.E.   L.E.A.D

DAY #61

ISAIAH 54:17

NEW INTERNATIONAL VERSION

17 no weapon forged against you will prevail,
and you will refute every tongue that accuses you.
This is the heritage of the servants of the LORD,
and this is their vindication from me,"
declares the LORD.

PRAYER
■■■

Father God in the name of Jesus Lord Teach me how to love
people behind the bars. Show me how to love them with faults.
Show me how to love by not judging. Show me how to love all
God's Children no matter what they have done. No matter what
is going on in their lives I need to love people where they are at
in their lives. Lord show me in Jesus' name Amen

****

AFFIRMATION

Author Zipporah Israel

I am beautiful inside
and out
. I make others happy
. I am respectful
I am a money magnet
I attract abundance in
everything I do

PROVERBS 26:11-12

NEW INTERNATIONAL VERSION

[11] As a dog returns to its vomit,

so fools repeat their folly.

[12] Do you see a person wise in their own eyes?

There is more hope for a fool than for them.

PRAYER

****

Father God in the name of Jesus please teach me self-love. Teach me to love me in my own skin. Teach me how to look at myself from head to toe and love what I see, teach me how to embrace myself and love me from inside out in Jesus' name we pray amen.

AFFIRMATION

Kadian Palmer-Asemota

With out a storm there is no testimony, keep riding your storms

DAY # 63

2 PETER 2:22

NEW INTERNATIONAL VERSION

[22] Of them the proverbs are true: "A dog returns to its vomit,"[a] and, "A sow that is washed returns to her wallowing in the mud."

PRAYER

****

Father God please help me love my inner self. Teach me to love my mind, my dreams, love my goals, love everything and anything about Pamela. In Jesus name I pray amen.

****

AFFIRMATION

Kadian Palmer-Asemota

Don't let your pain take away your

DAY #64

PHILIPPIANS 3:13

NEW INTERNATIONAL VERSION

[13] Brothers and sisters, I do not consider myself yet to have taken hold of it. But one thing I do: Forgetting what is behind and straining toward what is ahead,

PRAYER

****

Father God in the name of Jesus Thank you for teaching me how to love myself. Jesus thank you for teaching me self-love which we need to know how to do. In Jesus name Amen

****

AFFIRMATION

Kadian Palmer-
Asemota

. Why worry when God never gave up an you

DAY #65

REVELATION 3:19

NEW INTERNATIONAL VERSION

[19] Those whom I love I rebuke and discipline. So be earnest and repent.

PRAYER

****

Father God in the name of Jesus thank you for the love of our site. We take that for granted but I thank you for how I can see. With my eyes. With my spiritual eyes, and my vision. Thank you for allowing me to see the beauty of the trees, the flowers, the birds, all the scenery that Jesus that you create for us to see. Thank you, lord, in Jesus' name I pray amen.

AFFIRMATION

Kadian Palmer-Asemota

From nothing to something, you can do this.

DAY # 66

PROVERBS 12:15

NEW INTERNATIONAL VERSION

[15] The way of fools seems right to them,
but the wise listen to advice.

PRAYER

****

Father God in the name of Jesus for the love of taste. Thank you
for allowing us to taste all the amazing foods, candies, you allow
us to taste and experience. Thank you for the power of our
tongue for taste and to talk. In Jesus name amen

****

AFFIRMATION

Keywana Wright-
Jones

I have the
victory

DAY #67

PROVERBS 18:15

NEW INTERNATIONAL VERSION

[15] The heart of the discerning acquires knowledge,
for the ears of the wise seek it out.

PRAYER
■■

Father God in the name of Jesus thank you for allowing me the
scent of touch. Thank you for the power of the touch. Thank
you for allowing us to have hands, arms, fingers. I love how we
can feel different textures, how we can feed ourselves, take care
of ourselves, by taking a bath, cooking, cleaning, feeling each
other, the power of touch is amazing. Thank you, Lord in Jesus
name Amen.

****

AFFIRMATION

Keywana Wright-Jones

Don't let no one change your mind. If God said it that settles it.

LUKE 2:40

NEW INTERNATIONAL VERSION

[40] And the child grew and became strong; he was filled with wisdom, and the grace of God was on him.

PRAYER

****

Father God thank you for the love of the use of my legs & feet. Thank you for the power of walking and feeling with my feet. Thank you for allowing me to walk and the use of my legs, and feet. Thank you for allowing me the power of walking. How we can swim and be in the water and on land. In Jesus name I pray Amen.
■■

AFFIRMATION

Keywana Wright-Jones

God will take care of you.

L.E.A.R.N.   L.O.V.E.   L.E.A.D

DAY # 69

1 PETER 2:2-3

NEW INTERNATIONAL VERSION

[2] Like newborn babies, crave pure spiritual milk, so that by it you may grow up in your salvation, [3] now that you have tasted that the Lord is good

PRAYER

****

Father God in the name of Jesus thank for the love of sound with my ears. Thank you, lord, for allowing me to hear the sound of my voice. Thank you for allowing me to hear the sounds you have created in the world. Thank you for the sound of all animals, the sound of nature. I love to just listen to the beautiful music you make with thunder, and rain fall. That is a blessing. Thank you, Jesus, in your name I pray amen

****

AFFIRMATION

Keywana Wright-Jones

I will find rest in the Lord.

L.E.A.R.N.   L.O.V.E.   L.E.A.D

DAY #70

PROVERBS 3:1

NEW INTERNATIONAL VERSION

Wisdom Bestows Well-Being

3 My son, do not forget my teaching,
but keep my commands in your heart,

PRAYER

****

Father God in the name of Jesus thank you for the love of smell.
My nose. Thank you for allowing me to be able to smell the
millions of scents in the world. Thank you in Jesus' name Amen.

****

AFFIRMATION

**Keywana Wright-
Jones**

I will
remain
humble

DAY #71

PROVERBS 4:5

NEW INTERNATIONAL VERSION

[5] Get wisdom, get understanding;
do not forget my words or turn away from them.

PRAYER

****

Father God thank you for the love of my sisters that re praying with me on this journey. Thank you for the love that Angela gives unconditionally. Thank you for giving her this assignment and she sharing the love with me. Thank you for allowing us to grow stronger in this prayer journey. In Jesus name I pray amen.

****

AFFIRMATION

Keywana Wright-Jones

I must obey God to receive the blessing

DAY # 72

PHILIPPIANS 4:9

NEW INTERNATIONAL VERSION

[9] Whatever you have learned or received or heard from me, or seen in me—put it into practice. And the God of peace will be with you.

PRAYER
■■■

Father God thank you for the love of having a husband for the third time. But this love Jesus I know its correct because you were in the mist from start to now. The way we met, the way we read the one-year holy bible together, the way the day of our wedding you gave me a sign on the Saturday, January 11,2020 the weather was 70 degrees which was the sign you gave me to let me know yes, I was supposed to marry him. Thank you, lord, for giving me a life partner to love me, to protect me, to be my best friend, for me to teacher him the love of the lord. Thank you, lord, in Jesus' name Amen

****

AFFIRMATION

Keywana Wright-Jones

Cloud will come and rain will fall, but after while the sun will shine

DAY #73

PSALM 32:8

NEW INTERNATIONAL VERSION

[8] I will instruct you and teach you in the way you should go;
I will counsel you with my loving eye on you.

PRAYER

****

Father God in the name of Jesus thank you for the love of my parents. They taught me unconditional love first. They taught me the love of family. Thank you for showing me how to love my family unconditionally in Jesus' name Amen.

AFFIRMATION

Keywana Wright-Jones

God is making away for me

DAY #74

1 THESSALONIANS 5:11

NEW INTERNATIONAL VERSION

¹¹ Therefore encourage one another and build each other up, just as in fact you are doing.

PRAYER

****

Father God in the name Jesus thank you for the love of friendship. Friendships become your family that love of friendship is pure, its amazing, it grows. 2:02 PMhank you Jesus for the love of friendship on Jesus' name Amen.

****

AFFIRMATION

Keywana Wright-Jones

God will lead you step by step if you ask

PROVERBS 1:7

NEW INTERNATIONAL VERSION

[7] The fear of the LORD is the beginning of knowledge,
but fools[a] despise wisdom and instruction.

PRAYER

****

Father God in the name of Jesus thank you for the love of sisterhood.
Sisters can be by blood or you find each other by choice. Sisterly love is
beautiful and needed. Thank you for the love of sisterhood Amen.

****

AFFIRMATION

Keywana Wright-
Jones

When God
says move, you
must move

DAY #76

PSALM 25:4

NEW INTERNATIONAL VERSION

4 Show me your ways, LORD,
teach me your paths.

PRAYER

****

Father God in the name of Jesus thank you for showing the love
of a church family. That is some powerful love. Praying love,
healing love, community love. Thank you love for church love
in Jesus' name. Amen.

****

AFFIRMATION

Sandra Gamble

If you are going to be
a Prisoner! Be a
Prisoner of Hope!
Expectation is the
breeding ground for
Miracles!

DAY #77

PSALM 25:5

NEW INTERNATIONAL VERSION

⁵ Guide me in your truth and teach me,

for you are God my Savior,

and my hope is in you all day long.

PRAYER

****

Father God in the name of Jesus Lord thank you for the love of myself. Thank you for teaching me how to love myself. Thank you for teaching me how to love everything about myself. If I don't know how to love me Jesus how can I love others. Thank you for self-love in Jesus' name Amen.

AFFIRMATION

Sandra Gamble

I

AM A

HOPE

DEALER

DAY #78

PROVERBS 12:1

NEW INTERNATIONAL VERSION

12 Whoever loves discipline loves knowledge,

but whoever hates correction is stupid

PRAYER

■■

Father God in the name of Jesus thank you Lord for showing me
how to love mankind. Showing me how to humble myself.
Thank you for showing how to love everyone how you love us
unconditional. Everyone you have taught me need love. Thank
you, Jesus, in your name Amen.

AFFIRMATION

QUEEN ANGELA

TODAY I LEAD IN LOVE

TODAY ALLOW MY
ACTIONS TO SPEAK FOR
ME

L.E.A.R.N.   L.O.V.E.   L.E.A.D

DAY #79

DEUTERONOMY 8:5

NEW INTERNATIONAL VERSION

⁵ Know then in your heart that as a man disciplines his son, so the LORD your God disciplines you.

PRAYER

****

Father God in the name of Jesus' lord love is a powerful word. Love is an action word. Jesus, you taught me that its not just saying the words, you have to put action behind it. Thank you, Jesus. In your name Jesus, I love you Lord the way you never turn your back on me. I love you Jesus for always by my side. Jesus thank you for loving me by my side every step even when I didn't know you Jesus. Thank you in Jesus' name I pray Amen.

AFFIRMATION

QUEEN ANGELA

TODAY

I SPEAK L.I.F.E.

OVER MYSELF

GOD'S WILL FOR ME

DAY # 80

ACTS 20:20

NEW INTERNATIONAL VERSION

[20] You know that I have not hesitated to preach anything that would be helpful to you but have taught you publicly and from house to house.

PRAYER

****

Father God in the name of Jesus. Love Jesus thank you for allowing me to find Love. Thank you for allowing me to feel love. Thank you, Jesus, for teaching me how to love in Jesus' name Amen.

****

AFFIRMATION

Dominique E. Jones

If you're blessed to be different, don't ever change

DAY #81

LUKE 2:40

NEW INTERNATIONAL VERSION

[40] And the child grew and became strong; he was filled with wisdom, and the grace of God was on him.

PRAYER

****

Father God in the name of Jesus thank you for showing me the love of creativity. Thank you for giving the love of being able to imagine beautiful worlds and dreams, translate it to paper and share it to the world. Thank you for allowing me to become an author. I love to write and you taught me how to love my craft. In Jesus name amen.

****

AFFIRMATION

Dominique E. Jones

Always remember...someone 's effort is a reflection of their interest in you

DAY #82

PROVERBS 4:2

NEW INTERNATIONAL VERSION

[2] I give you sound learning,
so do not forsake my teaching

PRAYER

****

Father God in the name of Jesus God is love.　Love is God.
Thank you for your love thank you for never leaving my side.
Thank you, Lord.　Just thank you for loving me.　And teaching
me that I am always going to be love by you no matter what
thank you Lord. Jesus' name Amen.

AFFIRMATION

Dominique E. Jones

As you grow, don't forget the ones that helped deep root you.

DAY # 83

PROVERBS 9:9

NEW INTERNATIONAL VERSION

[9] Instruct the wise and they will be wiser still;
teach the righteous and they will add to their learning.

PRAYER

****

Father God in the name of Jesus Thank you for showing us how
to love animals. Thank you for the love of animals. They have
healing power for a lot of people who are lonely. The love of an
animals, help children learn how to take care love ones and
responsibility. The love of animals is a beautiful thing. Thank
you, Jesus, for showing so many ways to love in Jesus' name.
Amen.

****

AFFIRMATION

Dominique E.
Jones

Stay kind. It makes
you beautiful

DAY #84

TITUS 2:1

NEW INTERNATIONAL VERSION

2 You, however, must teach what is appropriate to sound doctrine.

PRAYER

****

Father God in the name of Jesus thank you for showing the love the church. The church is our family as well. Families are messy, they fight, they cry together, feel hope together, pray together and we will take care of our family. We take care of our own. Thank you, Jesus, for the love of the church. In Jesus name Amen.

****

AFFIRMATION

Dominique E. Jones

Your journey will help others heal...remember that when you feel like you're tapped

DAY #85

PROVERBS 22:6

NEW INTERNATIONAL VERSION

⁶ Start children off on the way they should go,
and even when they are old they will not turn from it.

PRAYER

****

Father God in the name of Jesus thank you for the love of family.
Thank you teaching how to our family when we do not like them.
Thank you for teaching us how to love our family when we are
sad. Teaching us how to love our family when we are hurting.
Thank you for teaching our family in times of sorrow. Thank
you, Jesus, for the love of family in Jesus' name Amen.

AFFIRMATION

Dominique E. Jones

People are blessed just because you showed up

DAY # 86

ROMANS 15:4

NEW INTERNATIONAL VERSION

⁴ For everything that was written in the past was written to teach us, so that through the endurance taught in the Scriptures and the encouragement they provide we might have hope.

PRAYER

****

Father God in the name of Jesus thank you for the love of Christ. Thank you, Jesus, for loving me. Loving me with all of my faults, my mistakes, my pain, my faith not being as strong as it should be, thank you Jesus for always loving me in Jesus' name I pray Amen.

AFFIRMATION
■■■

Dominique E. Jones

Magnify the small victories, not everyone knows how much that took

DAY #87

PROVERBS 10:7

NEW INTERNATIONAL VERSION

[7] The name of the righteous is used in blessings,[a]
but the name of the wicked will rot.

PRAYER

****

Father God in the name of Jesus thank you for the love of
friends. I thank you for placing people in my life that will love
me and remove people that I believed that loved me and was
doing right by me. Thank you, Jesus, for loving me in all of
these situations. In Jesus name we pray Amen.

****

AFFIRMATION

Dominique E. Jones
Not all strength is
physical...mental strength
is stronger than any
muscle you have

223

L.E.A.R.N.   L.O.V.E.   L.E.A.D

DAY #88

PSALM 32:8

NEW INTERNATIONAL VERSION

⁸ I will instruct you and teach you in the way you should go;
I will counsel you with my loving eye on you

PRAYER

****

Father God in the name of Jesus thank you for showing me how to love myself. Thank you, Jesus, for teaching me the importance of self-love. Thank you for teaching me to love myself and to put my heart first. Thank you, Jesus, in your son's name Amen.

****

AFFIRMATION

Dominique E. Jones

Start where you are. Use what you have. Do what you can.

224

DAY # 89

JAMES 1:5

NEW INTERNATIONAL VERSION

⁵ If any of you lacks wisdom, you should ask God, who gives generously to all without finding fault, and it will be given to you.

PRAYER

****

Father God in the name of Jesus thank you lord for the love of my children. Thank you for allowing me to be a parent. Thank you for allowing me to be a parent and experiencing love from my children. These and all blessings I ask in. Jesus' name Amen.

****

AFFIRMATION

Dominique E. Jones

If you're blessed to be different, don't ever change

DAY #90

JOHN 14:26

NEW INTERNATIONAL VERSION

²⁶ But the Advocate, the Holy Spirit, whom the Father will send in my name, will teach you all things and will remind you of everything I have said to you

PRAYER

****

Father God in the name. of Jesus thank you for teaching me how to love once I was hurt. Thank you for teaching to trust love with people again. Thank you, Jesus, for teaching me love after my heart was shattered. Thank you in Jesus' name Amen.

****

AFFIRMATION

Dominique E. Jones

Make them stop and stare. You're too authentic to walk past

MATTHEW 28:19-20

NEW INTERNATIONAL VERSION

[19] Therefore go and make disciples of all nations, baptizing them in the name of the Father and of the Son and of the Holy Spirit, [20] and teaching them to obey everything I have commanded you. And surely I am with you always, to the very end of the age."

PRAYER

****

Father God in the name of Jesus thank you for showing me the love of strangers. Thank you for showing me how to love people for who they are. Thank you, Jesus. In Jesus name I pray amen.

****

AFFIRMATION

Dominique E. Jones

Remind yourself what you've been able to overcome. You're more powerful then you think

227

PSALM 25:4

NEW INTERNATIONAL VERSION

⁴ Show me your ways, LORD,

teach me your paths.

PRAYER

****

Father God in the name of Jesus thank you for the love of my sons. Thank you for the love I feel as a parent. Thank you for the love of my sons. Thank you for allowing me to experience the love of a child. In Jesus word I pray amen.

AFFIRMATION

Dominique E. Jones

You may have some scars but who doesn't? The only difference is yours are visible

DAY #93

1 CORINTHIANS 13:4-5

NEW INTERNATIONAL VERSION

[4] Love is patient, love is kind. It does not envy, it does not boast, it is not proud. [5] It does not dishonor others, it is not self-seeking, it is not easily angered, it keeps no record of wrongs.

PRAYER

****

Father God in the name of Jesus thank you for self-love. Thank you for teaching me how to love myself. Thank you for teaching me that I am your daughter, and I am worthy of your love. Thank you, Jesus, in your name I pray amen.

****

AFFIRMATION

Dominique E. Jones

Like who you are but love who you're becoming

229

DAY #94

1 CORINTHIANS 13:6-8

NEW INTERNATIONAL VERSION

⁶ Love does not delight in evil but rejoices with the truth. ⁷ It always protects, always trusts, always hopes, always perseveres.

⁸ Love never fails. But where there are prophecies, they will cease; where there are tongues, they will be stilled; where there is knowledge, it will pass away.

PRAYER

****

Father God in the name of Jesus thank you for the love of nature. Thank you for your beautiful gifts of the power of sight, the power of smell, power of touch, power of taste, thank you for the love of the senses. In Jesus name I pray amen.

AFFIRMATION

Dominique E. Jones

Breathe. You've come out of things that you never knew you had the strength for. Don't doubt yourself this time

DAY # 95

1 JOHN 4:7-9

NEW INTERNATIONAL VERSION

7 Dear friends, let us love one another, for love comes from God. Everyone who loves has been born of God and knows God. 8 Whoever does not love does not know God, because God is love. 9 This is how God showed his love among us: He sent his one and only Son into the world that we might live through him.

PRAYER

****

Father God in the name of Jesus thank you for your love. Thank you for loving me through my pain. Thank you for loving me for loving when I have fallen. Thank you so much lord in Jesus name I pray Amen.

AFFIRMATION

Dominique E. Jones
I'm not lazy. I'm a warrior. I fight a fight that you'll never understand

231

DAY #96

ROMANS 5:8

NEW INTERNATIONAL VERSION

8 But God demonstrates his own love for us in this: While we were still sinners, Christ died for us.

PRAYER

****

Father God in the name of Jesus thank you lord for giving us hope. Thank you for allowing us to know your love that we know it's always hope for any situation. Thank you, Jesus, for your love. In Jesus name Amen.

AFFIRMATION

Dominique E. Jones

Grow so strong on the inside that nothing on the outside can affect your inner self

232

DAY #97

1 JOHN 3:18

NEW INTERNATIONAL VERSION

[18] Dear children, let us not love with words or speech but with actions and in truth.

PRAYER

****

Father God in the name of Jesus thank you for the love of people. Thank you for the love that we share with people we do not know. Thank you for allowing us to love and bring people into our circle with love. Thank. You in Jesus name Amen.

AFFIRMATION

Dominique E. Jones
Your last fight made you even stronger for this...and you didn't even realize it

DAY # 98

PROVERBS 10:12

NEW INTERNATIONAL VERSION

[12] Hatred stirs up conflict,

but love covers over all wrongs.

PRAYER

****

Father God in the name of Jesus thank you for the love of Jesus

thought sickness. Thank. You for loving us while we are sick

and you love us thought it. You Lord allow us to know that there

is hope even in our darkest hour. Thank you, Lord for Love. In

Jesus name Amen

AFFIRMATION

Dominique E. Jones

Dare to thank God
even it doesn't make
sense

DAY #99

1 Corinthians 16:14

New International Version

[14] Do everything in love.

PRAYER

****

Father God in the name of Jesus thank you Lord for the Love of patience's. Thank you for teaching us how to wait and take our situations to you Lord in prayer. Thank. You lord in Jesus name amen.

****

AFFIRMATION

Dominique E. Jones

If it doesn't get better, you get better

DAY #100

1 PETER 4:8

NEW INTERNATIONAL VERSION

[8] Above all, love each other deeply, because love covers over a multitude of sins.

PRAYER

****

Father God in the name Jesus thank you for self love. Thank you for teaching us self love. How to love ourselves in Jesus name amen.

****

AFFIRMATION

QUEEN ANGELA
I AM
PASSIONATE

DAY # 101

ROMANS 12:9-10

NEW INTERNATIONAL VERSION

[9] Love must be sincere. Hate what is evil; cling to what is good. [10] Be devoted to one another in love. Honor one another above yourselves.

PRAYER

****

Father God in the name of Jesus thank you for the love of people. Thank you allowing people of all walks of life to just open their hearts and love each other because of the of Jesus. Thank you in Jesus' name amen.

****

AFFIRMATION

QUEEN ANGELA
I AM
CARING

L.E.A.R.N.   L.O.V.E.   L.E.A.D

DAY #102

ROMANS 13:10

NEW INTERNATIONAL VERSION

[10] Love does no harm to a neighbor. Therefore, love is the fulfillment of the law

PRAYER

****

Father God in the name of Jesus thank you lord for love. Thank you for creating that feeling of love thank you for love. Amen.

****

AFFIRMATION

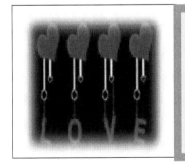

QUEEN
ANGELA
I AM
ADORED

L.E.A.R.N.   L.O.V.E.   L.E.A.D

DAY #103

MARK 12:31

NEW INTERNATIONAL VERSION

[31] The second is this: 'Love your neighbor as yourself.'[a] There is no commandment greater than these.

PRAYER by Cheniera Osbourne

****

Lord Open Up Doors For Your People Show Them Favor In Your Name Father. Amen

****

AFFIRMATION

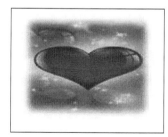

QUEEN ANGELA
I AM
CHARMING

DAY # 104

1 PETER 5:6-7

NEW INTERNATIONAL VERSION

[6] Humble yourselves, therefore, under God's mighty hand, that he may lift you up in due time. [7] Cast all your anxiety on him because he cares for you.

PRAYER by Cheniera Osbourne

****

Father God Bless My Family In A Special Way Remove Anything That's Not Of You Remove It Right Now In Jesus Name Amen.

****

AFFIRMATION

QUEEN ANGELA
I AM A RARE
GEM

DAY #105

PROVERBS 3:3-4

NEW INTERNATIONAL VERSION

[3] Let love and faithfulness never leave you;
bind them around your neck,
write them on the tablet of your heart.
[4] Then you will win favor and a good name
in the sight of God and man.

PRAYER by Cheniera Osbourne

****

Heal My Husband Body Lord Turn His Kidneys Into New
Kidneys In Your Mighty Name Amen. Father heal our land in the
name of Jesus.

****

AFFIRMATION

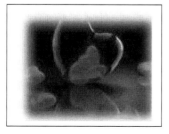

QUEEN ANGELA
I AM

CHERISHED

L.E.A.R.N.   L.O.V.E.   L.E.A.D

DAY #106

Luke 6:31

New International Version

³¹ Do to others as you would have them do to you.

PRAYER by Cheniera Osbourne

****

I Pray For My Son Who In Prison For 25 Years Over A
Backpack And No One Got Killed Or Hurt That God Remove
Them Years And Turn Them Into His Testimony For Your Will
God. Father thank You
■■I

AFFIRMATION

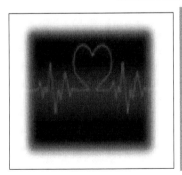

QUEEN ANGELA

I AM A

G.I.F.T.

FROM GOD

DAY # 107

PROVERBS 3:3-4

NEW INTERNATIONAL VERSION

[3] Let love and faithfulness never leave you;
bind them around your neck,
write them on the tablet of your heart.
[4] Then you will win favor and a good name
in the sight of God and man

PRAYER by Cheniera Osbourne

Lord Release My Nephew From Prison And Turn His Life
Around To Teach Other Young To Stay On The Right Path In
Jesus Name Amen

****

AFFIRMATION

QUEEN ANGELA
I AM
PURPOSED
FOR THIS

L.E.A.R.N.   L.O.V.E.   L.E.A.D

DAY #108

PSALM 86:15

NEW INTERNATIONAL VERSION

[15] But you, Lord, are a compassionate and gracious God,
slow to anger, abounding in love and faithfulness.

PRAYER by Cheniera Osbourne

****

Lord Heal Your Land And Keep Your Arms Around Your
People In Jesus Name.

****

AFFIRMATION

QUEEN ANGELA

I AM FREE TO BE

I AM FREE TO CREATE

I AM FREE TO LOVE

L.E.A.R.N.   L.O.V.E.   L.E.A.D

DAY #109

1 JOHN 4:12

NEW INTERNATIONAL VERSION

[12] No one has ever seen God; but if we love one another, God lives in us and his love is made complete in us

PRAYER by Cheniera Osbourne

****

Father God Watch Over My Daughters And Show Them Favor In Jesus Name.

AFFIRMATION

QUEEN ANGELA

I AM

FEARFULLY

&

WONDERFULLY

DESIGNED IN

HIS IMAGE FOR HIS GLORY

245

L.E.A.R.N.   L.O.V.E.   L.E.A.D

DAY # 110

JOHN 13:34

NEW INTERNATIONAL VERSION

[34] "A new command I give you: Love one another. As I have loved you, so you must love one another.

PRAYER by Cheniera Osbourne

****

Lord Continue To Let Me Do Your Work And Show Your People How Powerful You Are Amen.

****

AFFIRMATION

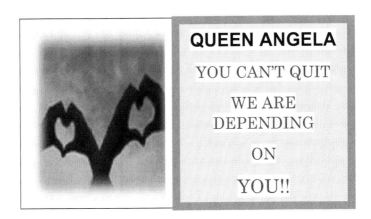

QUEEN ANGELA
YOU CAN'T QUIT
WE ARE
DEPENDING
ON
YOU!!

DAY #111

LEVITICUS 19:18

NEW INTERNATIONAL VERSION

[18] "'Do not seek revenge or bear a grudge against anyone among your people, but love your neighbor as yourself. I am the LORD.

PRAYER by Cheniera Osbourne

****

Lord I thank you for keeping watch over us as we be about this world. We thank you in advance for all you are doing . We thank you for opening and closing doors in the name of Jesus.

I

Thank You

Amen.

****

AFFIRMATION

QUEEN ANGELA
DON'T GIVE UP ON GOD,
HE HASN'T GIVEN UP ON YOU..

L.E.A.R.N. L.O.V.E. L.E.A.D

DAY #112

PROVERBS 17:17

NEW INTERNATIONAL VERSION

¹⁷ A friend loves at all times,
and a brother is born for a time of adversity.

PRAYER by Angela

****

Father I thank you with everything in me.

Continue to line me up with your word that I may be a willing vessel to be used by you! In Jesus name.

****

AFFIRMATION

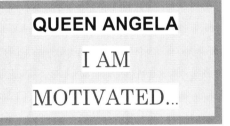

QUEEN ANGELA

I AM

MOTIVATED...

DAY # 113

MATTHEW 22:37

NEW INTERNATIONAL VERSION

[37] Jesus replied: "'Love the Lord your God with all your heart and with all your soul and with all your mind.'

PRAYER by Angela

****

Father I thank you for renewing my mind and keep me stayed on you.

Father guard my heart, mind and soul, no hurt harm or danger shall come nah me.

AFFIRMATION

QUEEN ANGELA
I AM EVOLVING
INTO WHOM GOD
CREATED ME TO BE

DAY #114

ROMANS 13:8

NEW INTERNATIONAL VERSION

[8] Let no debt remain outstanding, except the continuing debt to love one another, for whoever loves others has fulfilled the law.

PRAYER by Angela

****

Father let not my heart be troubled,

Father allow my truth to be a light to someone.

Love is action allow my actions to speak for me on this journey and I will be sure to give you GLORY!!

AFFIRMATION

QUEEN ANGELA
I AM OWNING
MY
T.R.U.T.H.S.

DAY #115

PSALM 143:8

NEW INTERNATIONAL VERSION

[8] Let the morning bring me word of your unfailing love,

for I have put my trust in you.

Show me the way I should go,

for to you I entrust my life.

PRAYER by Angela

****

Father show me the way, father in Jesus' name.

AFFIRMATION

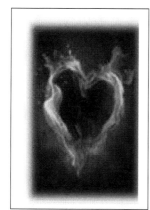

QUEEN ANGELA
T.R.U.T.H.S.

T-TEST, TRIALS &
TRIBULATIONS

R- RESILIENCE

U-UNIQUENESS

T-TRANSPARENCY

L.E.A.R.N.   L.O.V.E.   L.E.A.D

DAY # 116

GALATIANS 5:13

NEW INTERNATIONAL VERSION

[13] You, my brothers and sisters, were called to be free. But do not use your freedom to indulge the flesh[a]; rather, serve one another humbly in love.

PRAYER by Angela

****

Father today I walk in freedom because you are yet ALIVE IN ME. Father keep me humble and steadfast on this path, never letting it be about me. In Jesus name this

****

AFFIRMATION

QUEEN ANGELA
I AM
P.O.W.E.R.ful

L.E.A.R.N.   L.O.V.E.   L.E.A.D

DAY #117

1 THESSALONIANS 3:12

NEW INTERNATIONAL VERSION

[12] May the Lord make your love increase and overflow for each other and
for everyone else, just as ours does for you

PRAYER by Angela

****

**Father today I walk in POWER because your love overflows in me and
I thank you for Loving me so much you sent your son Jesus to be an
example for us to live by. Father I thank you in Jesus name Amen ….**

****

AFFIRMATION

QUEEN ANGELA
P.O.W.E.R.
P-POSITIONED
O-OVERCOMER
W-WILLING VESSEL
E-EMPOWER
R-RESILENCE

L.E.A.R.N.   L.O.V.E.   L.E.A.D

DAY #118

1 JOHN 4:19

NEW INTERNATIONAL VERSION

¹⁹ We love because he first loved us.

PRAYER by Angela

****

Father

your will not mines, no weapon formed against me shall prosper. I am Destiny to Overcome because God has Positioned me here to Educate, Empower and Encourage others into their purpose. I shall not be moved. I will move in LOVE in Jesus name. Amen

****

AFFIRMATION

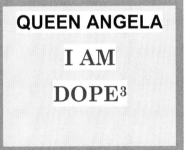

QUEEN ANGELA

I AM

DOPE³

254

L.E.A.R.N.   L.O.V.E.   L.E.A.D

DAY # 119

1 CORINTHIANS 13:13

NEW INTERNATIONAL VERSION

[13] And now these three remain: faith, hope and love. But the greatest of these is love.

PRAYER by Angela

****

Father today I have FAITH to not stop , HOPE to keep moving and understand that it's not my timing but God's timing and I'm reminded that in my waiting stage I have to LEARN TO LOVE MORE IN ORDER TO BECOME THAT LEADER HE HAS COLLED ME TO BE.   So while I wait father show me how to operate in AGAPE love. In Jesus name I pray. Amen

****

AFFIRMATION

QUEEN ANGELA

DOPE3

D-DESTINY   O-OVERCOMER

P-POSITIONED

E3 -EDUCATE, EMPOWER &
ENCOURAGE

255

L.E.A.R.N.   L.O.V.E.   L.E.A.D

DAY #120

JOHN 15:13

NEW INTERNATIONAL VERSION

[13] Greater love has no one than this: to lay down one's life for one's friends.

PRAYER by Angela

****

FATHER

I THANK YOU FOR SENDING YOU SON JESUS TO BE AN EXAMPLE OF HOW TO LIVE UPON THIS EARTH CONTINUE TO GUIDE AND LEAD US. YOUR WILL. IN JESUS NAME

****

AFFIRMATION

QUEEN ANGELA

I AM

S.T.R.O.N.G.

L.E.A.R.N.   L.O.V.E.   L.E.A.D

DAY #121

JOHN 3:16

NEW INTERNATIONAL VERSION

[16] For God so loved the world that he gave his one and only Son, that whoever believes in him shall not perish but have eternal life

PRAYER by Angela

****

FATHER

KEEP ME FOCUSED when the cares of this world become more than my flesh can handle, extend your strength and endurance to my spirit man to continue on this journey. Father never allow me or my feelings guide, instruct or lead your people astray.

Keep STAYED ON YOU IN JESUS NAME

****

AFFIRMATION

QUEEN ANGELA

YOU ARE STRONG

S-STRNGTH   T-TRANSPARECNY

R- RESILENCE   O-OVERCOMER

N-NEXT LEVEL   G- GOD FIRST

257

L.E.A.R.N.   L.O.V.E.   L.E.A.D

MY PRAYER IS THAT OVER THE
NEXT 121 DAYS YOU WILL BE
BLESSED FROM THE PRAYERS
& AFFIRMATIONS SHARED ON
THESE PAGES. MAY THESE
WORDS BECOME LIFE AND
SPEAK TO YOUR HEART, MIND
AND S.O.U.L.

LEAD

L- Willing to Learn, always a teachable student.

E- Etiquette & Poise to handle the world without being of the world.

A- Helping others Activate thru the word of God their purpose.

D- Disciplines of the gospel, always willing to teach, lead and preach the word.

Angela Thomas Smith
(Queen Of Collaboration)

caring, compassionate. down2earth.loving.out going,
family/community oriented, co-author of 22 books.

261

L.E.A.R.N.   L.O.V.E.   L.E.A.D

DAY # 1

Deuteronomy 4:27

King James Version

27 And the Lord shall scatter you among the nations, and ye shall be left few in number among the heathen, whither the Lord shall lead you.

PRAYER

****

Father I pray that you will watch over your word today in our lives as we go & share across the nation your gospel for the building of your kingdom.

****

AFFIRMATION

Rolanda T Pyle

Service to others is the rent we pay to live on earth. Give and it will come back to you!

DAY #2

Judges 5:12

New International Version

[12] 'Wake   up, wake   up,   Deborah!

Wake   up,   wake   up,   break   out   in   song!

Arise,   Barak!

Take captive your captives, son of Abinoam.'

PRAYER

****

Father I thank you for this day that was not yet promised us.
Father you said in your word that you would never leave us nor
forsake us . I thank you for allowing us this time to come before
you , to find me in you.

****

AFFIRMATION

Queen Angela
I HAVE PURPOSE
JEREMIAH 29:11 REMINDS ME OF THAT

DAY #3

Psalm 5:8

New International Version

[8] Lead me, LORD, in your righteousness
because of my enemies—
make your way straight before me.

PRAYER

****

Father I thank you for the mind to seek you . I thank you for the
heart to thirst for you. I thank you for Jeremiah 29:11 your word
reminds me that you said you had a plan for me.

AFFIRMATION

Queen Angela

I HAVE P.O.W.E.R. BECAUSE I
AM A PRODUCT OF THE MOST
HIGH MADE IN HIS IMAGE

DAY # 4

Psalm 25:5

New International Version

[5] Guide me in your truth and teach me,
for you are God my Savior,
and my hope is in you all day long

PRAYER

****

Father I thank you for touching my heart, mind and soul to seek after you and your truth. Lord, I thank you for saving me from me and the traps of the world to keep me from doing your will and walking in your purpose for my life.

■■■

AFFIRMATION

Queen Angela

I WOKE UP THIS DAY

I AM BLESSED

265

DAY #5

Psalm 27:11

New International Version

[11] Teach me your way, LORD;
lead me in a straight path
because of my oppressors.

PRAYER

****

Father, please keep me steadfast in your word. Teach and guide
me daily that my flesh may come under submission to your will
for my life.

****

AFFIRMATION

Queen Angela
I WILL WAIT UPON
THE LORD
HE IS MY STRENGTH

266

DAY #6

Psalm 31:3

New International Version

[3] Since you are my rock and my fortress,
for the sake of your name lead and guide me..

PRAYER

****

Father thanks for allow me to be on this journey we call LIFE. I thank you
for health and strength today.   Teach me thou ways oh lord not my way
allow my LIFE to be a living example.

AAFIRMATION

Queen Angela

I WILL

NOT BE

DEFEATED

DAY # 7

Psalm 43:3

New International Version

[3] Send me your light and your faithful care,
let them lead me;
let them bring me to your holy mountain,
to the place where you dwell.

PRAYER

****

**Father God in Jesus name, today I'm standing on your word.
You are my rock and for thy namesake lead and guide me oh
lord.**

AFFIRMATION

Queen Angela

IT STARTS WITH ME
TODAY I CHOOSE
ME.

DAY #8

Psalm 61:2

New International Version

^{2} From the ends of the earth I call to you,
I call as my heart grows faint;
lead me to the rock that is higher than I.

PRAYER

****

Lord when I don't understand, teach me. When I lack , you will provide. When I hurt, you shall heal me. Father I know you are all I have and desire. Keep me holy and accountable for the things of GOD.

****

AFFIRMATION

Queen Angela

I AM

FEARFULLY & WONDERFULLY

MADE

DAY #9

Psalm 143:10

New International Version

[10] Teach me to do your will,
for you are my God;
may your good Spirit
lead me on level ground.

PRAYER

****

Lead me, Guide me, Teach me to be more like you daily.
Allow my flesh to die to your subjection.

AFFIRMATION

Queen Angela

THIS JOY I HAVE THE WORLD DIDN'T GIVE IT THE WORLD CAN'T TAKE IT AWAY.

DAY # 10

Proverbs 8:20

New International Version

[20] I walk in the way of righteousness,
along the paths of justice

PRAYER

****

**Father only allow me to speak the truth. Lead me in the path
of righteousness   Equip me to walk and talk boldly the truth
of God. Only the truth no Sugar Coating.**

■■■

AFFIRMATION

Queen Angela
L.I.F.E.

L-LOVE

I-INSPIRATION

F-FEAR OF GOD

E- EDUCATE, EMPOWER & ENCOURAGE

DAY #11

Proverbs 6:22

New International Version

[22] When you walk, they will guide you;
when you sleep, they will watch over you;
when you awake, they will speak to you.

PRAYER

****

**Father I will keep showing up, I want stop. If you keep
waking me up I'll keep sharing your word every chance I get.
Lord cloth me in your righteousness in Jesus name.**

****

AFFIRMATION

Queen Angela

NO LONGER WILL I BE
SILENT

I HAVE A VOICE TO

SPEAK

DAY #12

Isaiah 42:16

New International Version

[16] I will lead the blind by ways they have not known,
along unfamiliar paths I will guide them;
I will turn the darkness into light before them
and make the rough places smooth.
These are the things I will do;
I will not forsake them.

PRAYER

****

Thy will not my will.

Keep me humble and stayed on you.

Continue to lead and guide us daily!

Move us out of the way.

AFFIRMATION

Queen Angela

ALL THINGS ARE POSSIBLE THRU CHRIST

DAY # 13

Isaiah 57:18

New International Version

[18] I have seen their ways, but I will heal them;
I will guide them and restore comfort to Israel's mourners,

PRAYER

****

**Father I thank you for this journey. I thank you for life,
health, and strength it hasn't been easy nor did I expect it to
be. Thanks for wrapping your arms around me. In Jesus
name.**

****

AFFIRMATION

Queen Angela

ALLOW HIS
LIGHT TO
SHINE
THRU

DAY #14

Luke 6:39

New International Version

³⁹ He also told them this parable: "Can the blind lead the blind? Will they not both fall into a pit?

PRAYER

****

Father I thank for yet another day to show me, me in your word. Father I thank your for this time to study your word, spend time with finding out who I am in you. Father thanks for opening my eyes and ears.

****

AFFIRMATION

Queen Angela

TODAY I MOVE OUT OF THE WAY AND ALLOW YOU TO LEAD ME

DAY #15

Matthew 15:14

New International Version

[14] Leave them; they are blind guides.[a] If the blind lead the blind, both will fall into a pit."

PRAYER

****

Father allow me to be bold when sharing the word. Keep me Holy and steadfast in your word. Thank you Jesu…..

AFFIRMATION

Queen Angela

I AM MORE THAN ENOUGH.

DAY # 16

Matthew 6:13

New International Version

¹³ And lead us not into temptation,[a]
but deliver us from the evil one.[b]'

PRAYER

****

**Father I thank you for your word on today. Lord I pray that
every scripture I read become living life to me. Father
anything not like you that will cause me not to be the leader
you have called me to be please BURN it out now.......
Father your word said you would not lead us into temptation,
but you would deliver us from evil. You also said you would
preserve thy going out and coming in. Lord I trust you to
lead me. I'm willing to be LEAD by you father.**

****

AFFIRMATION

Queen Angela

I AM THE
CHANGE
I DESIRE TO
SEE

DAY #17

Revelation 7:17

New International Version

[17] For the Lamb at the center of the throne
will be their shepherd;
'he will lead them to springs of living water.'[a]
'And God will wipe away every tear from their eyes.'

PRAYER

****

Father thanks for not forgetting about be me . Thank you for
chosen me . Thank you for being JEHOVAH-JIREH and when
we are sick you are JEHOVAH-ROPHE. Thank you for waking
me up and bring me understanding to your word.

****

AFFIRMATION

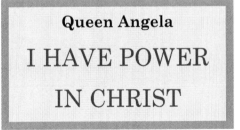

Queen Angela

I HAVE POWER
IN CHRIST

DAY #18

Psalm 23:3

New International Version

³ he refreshes my soul.

He guides me along the right paths

for his name's sake.

PRAYER

****

Father I thank you that my life shall be a living example of

how to be Holy and keep your commandments. Keep me

stayed on you . In Jesus name.

****

AFFIRMATION

Queen Angela

I AM WORTHY

Jeremiah 29:13

New International Version

[13] You will seek Me and find me when you seek me with all your heart.

PRAYER

****

Father I thank you for yet another chance to get it right.   I bind the spirit of fear and death. We are the Jesus nation. The kingdom of God is ready to the nation you have called us to be. I will trust you when I can't see you ... I will trust you when I can't trace you. Direct my path!!!!   In Jesus Name .....Keep me humble and steadfast on your word.....

AFFIRMATION

Queen Angela

I AM

HEALED .

DAY #20

Galatians 6:9

New International Version

[9] Let us not become weary in doing good, for at the proper time
we will reap a harvest if we do not give up.

PRAYER

****

**Father I will stand on your word no matter what it looks like
in the natural. You are my strength and my joy. I know you
will guide and lead me. In Jesus name!**

****

AFFIRMATION

Queen Angela

I AM A led by
the
Spirit of God

281

DAY #21

Philippians 2:3

New International Version

³ Do nothing out of selfish ambition or vain conceit. Rather, in humility value others above yourselves,

PRAYER

FATHER YOUR WILL NOT MINES IN JESUS NAME MOVE THRU ME TODAY THAT SOMEONE WILL SEE YOU IN ME. I THANK YOU IN ADVANCE.

****

AFFIRMATION

Dominique E. Jones
Forget all the reasons it didn't work and work on the one reason why it will

DAY # 22

Philippians 4:13

New International Version

[13] I can do all this through him who gives me strength.

PRAYER

****

Father, protect me from Me...

In Jesus name

AFFIRMATION

Queen Angela

NO TIME LIKE THE PRESENT TO CREATE IMPACT......

WHAT ARE YOU WAITING?...

LEGACY WAITS FOR NO ONE

DAY #23

Proverbs 27:23

New International Version

²³ Be sure you know the condition of your flocks,

give careful attention to your herds;

PRAYER

****

**Father I thank you for every woman connect to the l3
movement. Father bless them in a special way for their
commit to the project.**

****

AFFIRMATION

*Dominique E.
Jones*

Pain may always
there but suffering
is a choice

DAY #24

Luke 6:31

New International Version

[31] Do to others as you would have them do to you.

PRAYER

****

Father today I reminded that I am supposed to lead by example. That no matter how people treat me I am still to show love. When people see me I want them to see the Jesus in me. Father keep me faithful and steadfast in your word.

■■■

AFFIRMATION

Dominique E. Jones

The power of "no" will save your life...literally.

Matthew 20:26

New International Version

²⁶ Not so with you. Instead, whoever wants to become great among you must be your servant,

PRAYER

****

Father thanks for another day to come before you to touch and agree on behalf of your people today. Father we are seeking guidance and direction on how to navigate thru this earth realm. Father I pray every prayer that is lifted on today will bring you glory and work for our good. Father I thank you yet another opportunity to pour into someone's life and to make a difference.

****

AFFIRMATION

Dominique E. Jones

Make them stop and stare. You're too authentic to walk past without being noticed

DAY #26

Proverbs 29:11

New International Version

[11] Fools give full vent to their rage,
but the wise bring calm in the end

PRAYER
■■

Thanks for breathing breathe into me one more time. I
thank you for your word on today because it reminds me that
it's okay to hold my feelings back sometime rather than
venting like a fool. Lord thank you for strength to endure
and to stand.

****

AFFIRMATION

Dominique E. Jones

What you go through is
not about you,
remember that before
you try to take someone
else's hope away

DAY #27

Luke 22:26

New International Version

²⁶ But you are not to be like that. Instead, the greatest among you should be like the youngest, and the one who rules like the one who serve.

PRAYER

****

Father thanks for allowing me to serve. Thanks for giving me a serving spirit. Father keep me humble father remind me daily exactly why I am here. Never let it be about me. Father I fall don't let me stay down to long. Stir up your spirit that's in me. That I may live and not die.

****

AFFIRMATION

Dominique E. Jones

You're only limit is your mind

DAY # 28

Matthew 20:26

New International Version

[26] Not so with you. Instead, whoever wants to become great among you must be your servant,

PRAYER

****

Father I thank you yet for another day not promised me, but because you saw fit to breathe into me LIFE today, I yield to you to led by you. To be a great leader, I know I must be a great servant, Father teach me to serve with honor and grace. Lord give me a peace and joy that will never change despite my present moment. Thank you for you are evident and present in my life. In Jesus name AMEN.

****

AFFIRMATION

Dominique E. Jones

Everyone has their perks. Don't think because theirs looks different yours aren't wanted.

DAY #29

Mark 9:35

New International Version

³⁵ Sitting down, Jesus called the Twelve and said, "Anyone who wants to be first must be the very last, and the servant of all."

PRAYER

****

Thank you for this new day I never see before and will never see again. Thank you. Father allow your will to be done in my life and thru my life. I yield to you today bring my flesh under submission. Keep me holy and filled with your anointing. May someone see you thru me today.

AFFIRMATION

Dominique E. Jones

Stop shrinking into places you've outgrown

L.E.A.R.N.   L.O.V.E.   L.E.A.D

DAY #30

Hebrews 13:7

New International Version

[7] Remember your leaders, who spoke the word of God to you. Consider the outcome of their way of life and imitate their faith.

PRAYER

****

Father today I am reminded that you are my helper and I will not fear what man shall do unto me . Today I will be bold and intentional about the things of God. Father remove me and stir up my spirit man on today. Let me not walk by sight but by faith. In Jesus name amen…

AFFIRMATION

Dominique E. Jones

Today may be a bad day, but don't overlook the good day you just had.

DAY # 31

Romans 1:1

New International Version

1 Paul, a servant of Christ Jesus, called to be an apostle and set apart for the gospel of God—

PRAYER

****

Father today my desire is your desire for my life. My life isn't my life, its for your glory. Father guide me down the path of righteous and wholeness on today. Keep me lord. In Jesus name.

****

AFFIRMATION

Dominique E. Jones

Live life on purpose... with a purpose

DAY #32

Matthew 20:28

New International Version

[28] just as the Son of Man did not come to be served, but to serve, and to give his life as a ransom for many."

PRAYER

****

Father today as we go out into the world keep a watch over us. Keep us focused on you and your word, allow our lives to be an example for others to see you thru us and ask what they must do to be saved. Your will father not my will keep my flesh under submission.

■■■

AFFIRMATION

Dominique E. Jones

Don't let the only time you help someone be when you're good because someone helped you when they weren't

293

DAY #33

1 Timothy 4:12

New International Version

[12] Don't let anyone look down on you because you are young, but set an example for the believers in speech, in conduct, in love, in faith and in purity..

PRAYER

Father thanks for reminding me that it's not about a title or holding an office in the church but about being holy and living upright before the father. Father allow my life to a living example of the Jesus in me. Allow my actions to speak for me. In Jesus name your will shall be done.

****

AFFIRMATION

Dominique E. Jones

I don't adapt. I influence

DAY # 34

2 Timothy 2:15

New International Version

[15] Do your best to present yourself to God as one approved, a worker who does not need to be ashamed and who correctly handles the word of truth.

PRAYER

****

Today I just say thank you. Thank you Lord.... Thankyou Lord.... Thank you, Lord. If I had a million tongue, I could never thank you for you have truly been good to me. I am just grateful and humble for every person attached to this project father you move in their lives. Father bless them for not thinking it robbery to be apart of this movement. Blessings in Jesus name.

****

AFFIRMATION

Dominique E. Jones

Check your posture of heart when someone gets blessed before

DAY #35

Mark 10:45

New International Version

⁴⁵ For even the Son of Man did not come to be served, but to serve, and to give his life as a ransom for many."

PRAYER

****

Father I thank you for reminding me in your word that to LEAD you must be willing to serve. I thank you for the spirit of a servant, the willingness to give of my self and never be in competition with anyone. Thanks for giving me a heart for assisting your people. In Jesus name Amen

****

AFFIRMATION

Dominique E. Jones

Self evaluation is key. Check yourself so someone won't take credit for your progress

DAY #36

Isaiah 41:10

New International Version

[10] So do not fear, for I am with you;
do not be dismayed, for I am your God.
I will strengthen you and help you;
I will uphold you with my righteous right hand

PRAYER

**Father thanks for being my strength when I am weak.
Thanks for giving me the spirit of LOVE that covers a
multitude of sin.   I'm reminded that it's okay to fail but
don't stay down when you fall. Pick yourself up dust off and
keep pushing. Repent, Repair, Remove (Repeat until you get
it) God's time is not our time.   Father thanks for guidance in
Jesus' name.**

****

AFFIRMATION

Dominique E. Jones

Teach ppl how to handle
you, they've never dealt
with you before

297

John 3:30

New International Version

[30] He must become greater; I must become less.

PRAYER

****

FATHER HAVE YOUR WAY TODAY

BE LIGHT TO MY DARKNESS ON TODAY

**LORD EVERYTHING NOT OF YOU BURN IT OUT IN
JESUS NAME AMEN.**

AFFIRMATION

Dominique E. Jones

Show patience with
others, you're still
learning you

L.E.A.R.N.   L.O.V.E.   L.E.A.D

DAY #38

Matthew 7:12

New International Version

[12] So in everything, do to others what you would have them do to you, for this sums up the Law and the Prophets.

PRAYER

****

Father I thank you for being a present help to me, reminding me that I must give what I desire to receive. If I want love I have to show myself loveable. Father I than you for your word. I'm growing daily and getting a true understanding. Amen.

****

AFFIRMATION

Dominique E. Jones

Opinions are just that...don't define it as validation

299

DAY #39

Proverbs 4:23

New International Version

²³ Above all else, guard your heart,
for everything you do flows from it.

PRAYER

****

**FATHER TODAY KEEP ME INTENTIONAL ABOUT
THE THINGS OF YOU AND ONLY YOU.   IN JESUS
NAME**

****

AFFIRMATION

Dominique E. Jones

God gave us this life
for a reason, remind
him why

Proverbs 29:2

New International Version

2 When the righteous thrive, the people rejoice;
when the wicked rule, the people groan.

PRAYER

■■

I rejoice because the joy I have the world didn't give it the
world can't take it away. I will praise him when I can't see
him, I will praise him when I cant trace him. There is
nothing that will separate me from the love of God.

Amen amen amen

AFFIRMATION

Dr. Karen D. Lomax

I surround myself
with those who are
happy about my
happiness.

301

DAY #41

Acts 20:28

New International Version

[28] Keep watch over yourselves and all the flock of which the Holy Spirit has made you overseers. Be shepherds of the church of God,[a] which he bought with his own blood

PRAYER
■■■

Father I thank you for reminding me that I was fearfully and wonderfully made in your image. That I am more than enough and that I had the POWER manifest my destiny according to GENSIS 2:7 you breathe the breath of LIFE in me so a part of you is already in me. Father stir up those GIFTS that's already in me and allow me to be a light . Father your will…what is it you shall have me to do today. Father use me for your glory. Let it never be about me but my LIFE shall bring GLORY to your name. In Jesus name this is my prayer.

****

AFFIRMATION

Dr. Karen D. Lomax

I love myself enough to make ME a priority.

DAY #42

Mark 9:42

New International Version

[42] "If anyone causes one of these little ones—those who believe in me—to stumble, it would be better for them if a large millstone were hung around their neck and they were thrown into the sea.

PRAYER

Father thanks for this day that I will never see again. Allow me to move in your will today. Father distraction will come but keep me focused on you and the things of you. Never allow my flesh to be gloried. Father watch over those that are walking in darkness, continue to guide them until your marvelous light. Heal your people all over this land. Father whatever need that needs to be met on today lead us to where and who can help met that need for your GLORY!! I thank you for FAVOR on today!!!!

****

AFFIRMATION

Myra Armstead

Your life experiences are not meant to harm you. They are tools used by God to mold and shape you into the person he has called you to be.

DAY # 43

Psalm 124:2

New International Version

[2] if the LORD had not been on our side
when people attacked us,

PRAYER

****

THEE

WILL

NOT

**MY WILL LORD, I GIVE IT TO YOU TODAY. I
REALIZE I HAVE NO POWER THE ONLY POWER I
HAVE IS THRU YOU.**

AFFIRMATION

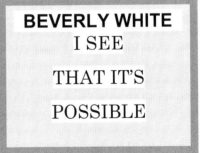

BEVERLY WHITE
I SEE
THAT IT'S
POSSIBLE

DAY #44

Psalm 125:1

New International Version

[1] Those who trust in the LORD are like Mount Zion,
which cannot be shaken but endures forever.

PRAYER

****

**Father thanks for not forgetting about me. Lord thank you
for converting my heart and lining me up to your word.
Lord keep me postured and positioned to walk upright in
Jesus name AMEN.**

****

AFFIRMATION

BEVERLY WHITE
**.I AM HERE IF YOU
NEED TO TALK. YOU
DON'T HAVE TO GO
THRU IT ALONE**

305

DAY #45

Psalm 127:1

New International Version

[1] Unless the LORD builds the house,
the builders labor in vain.
Unless the LORD watches over the city,
the guards stand watch in vain.

PRAYER

****

**Your will father, not my will. You didn't have to, but you
allowed me to see this new day. Father never let my journey
be about me but keep me focused on my purpose in Jesus
amen. Your Will father not mine Will.**

AFFIRMATION

BEVERLY WHITE
LET GO
MOVE FORWARD
AND LIVE

DAY # 46

Psalm 122:1

New International Version

[1] I rejoiced with those who said to me,
"Let us go to the house of the LORD."

PRAYER

****

**Father I thank you for this new day to draw closer to you.
his scripture reminds me of your willingness father to accept
me no matter where I am in Christ if I just repent and turn.
Father thanks for loving me more than I could every love my
self. Keep me humble in Jesus' name.**

****

AFFIRMATION

BEVERLY WHITE

**TO LEARN IS TO
GROW**

**LET'S GROW
TOGETHER**

Psalm 128:1

New International Version

[1] Blessed are all who fear the LORD,
who walk in obedience to him.

PRAYER

Father I thank you for LIFE and not just existing. Teach me how to LOVE more, unconditional love, how to be an inspiration to others. Direct my every step, let not my faith be shaken or moved. Father continue to fill me with your oil that I may be a lamp onto this dark dreary world. In Jesus name AMEN.

****

AFFIRMATION

JULIE THOMAS
Remember whether people listen and/or follow us

DAY #48

Psalm 120:1

New International Version

[1] I call on the LORD in my distress,
and he answers me.

PRAYER

****

Thank you, Lord, for ordering my steps, no matter what it looks like in nature. I trust your word on today father you are my present help. Father allow your light to shine through me that someone would want to be saved. Father thank you for waking me up to your truth, your word, and your way. I am grateful and thankful for Jesus.
Amen Amen amen

■■

AFFIRMATION

JULIE THOMAS

Go out into world and change it women

DAY #49

PSALM 134

NEW INTERNATIONAL VERSION

¹ Praise the LORD, all you servants of the LORD
who minister by night in the house of the LORD.
² Lift up your hands in the sanctuary
and praise the LORD.

³ May the LORD bless you from Zion,
he who is the Maker of heaven and earth

PRAYER

****

**Father I thank you for your word shall not return to
you void. Today I speak healing, father line our organs up to
function how you designed them to function. Father every
aliment that has come to bring distraction I bind it right now.
Father you said in your word we are heal and I speak healing
right now. I praise you because you are worth and deserving
of all our praise.**

AFFIRMATION

JULIE THOMAS
Remember
not to question
God's voice or word

L.E.A.R.N.   L.O.V.E.   L.E.A.D

DAY #50

PSALM 130:1-2

NEW INTERNATIONAL VERSION

[1]Out of the depths I cry to you, LORD;
[2] Lord, hear my voice.
Let your ears be attentive
to my cry for mercy.

PRAYER

****

Father I thank you for opening my eyes and ears that you my
reveal yourself to me. Father I thank for allowing me to be watchmen on the
wall for your people. Lord thanks for keeping me humble and steadfast on
your word. I will not be silent you have provided an opportunity for me to
use the gifts that you have placed on the inside of me. Father thanks for not
forget about me. In Jesus name I shall not be moved. Father you said in
Exodus 4:12 NOW THEREFORE GO AND I WILL BE WITH THY
MOUTH AND TEACH THEE WHAT THOU SHALL SAY. In Jesus name.

****

AFFIRMATION

Own Your
Purpose, On
Purpose.

Daphne
Hampton

DAY # 51

PROVERBS 1:5

NEW INTERNATIONAL VERSION

⁵ let the wise listen and add to their learning,
and let the discerning get guidance

PRAYER

****

Father today I speak healing to body. Father anything that is trying to attach itself to any part of our body I bind it right now. I come against cancerous cells, diabetes, high blood pressure. Father anything that is causing out bodies to not line up and function the way you have designed it. I bring it in line right now. We are healed in your son Jesus name. father I thank you because you have no respected person. What you do for one you will do for the rest. We are blessed and highly favor because you said so ... In Jesus name

****

AFFIRMATION

Purpose is an essential element.

Daphne Hampton

DAY #52

PROVERBS 3:1

NEW INTERNATIONAL VERSION

My son, do not forget my teaching,
but keep my commands in your heart,

PRAYER

****

Father, please allow me to keep the spirit of a student never thinking I had learned all I need to know. Keep me humbled that I may grow in love and others would want to know how and seek after the kingdom as well. Thank you for every day, that I get a chance to be a change maker and impact live.

AFFIRMATION

NO IS A VERY EMPOWERING WORD

Daphne Hampton

DAY #53

PROVERBS 6:22

NEW INTERNATIONAL VERSION

²² When you walk, they will guide you;
when you sleep, they will watch over you;
when you awake, they will speak to you

PRAYER

****

**Father thank you for setting me apart, calling and equipping
me for a time just as this. Your time is always the right time.
I thank you for loving me first. In Jesus name amen.**

AFFIRMATION

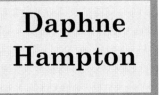

DAY # 54

PROVERBS 9:10

NEW INTERNATIONAL VERSION

[10] The fear of the LORD is the beginning of wisdom,

and knowledge of the Holy One is understanding.

PRAYER

**Father I thank you for waking me p in the spirit. I thank you
that I am no longer blind to your truth. Father I thank you
for the opportunity to share your word, your truth to your
people to help bring healing across the land. Father keep me
humble and focused on the purpose. I thank your for just
being who you are in our lives daily you extend your grace
and mercy.**

AFFIRMATION

Daphne
Hampton

WHEN YOU SEE
CRAZY COMING,
CROSS THE
STREET AND
JUMP THE FENCE!

Most Daphinatly

315

Proverbs 13:1

New International Version

13 A wise son heeds his father's instruction,
but a mocker does not respond to rebukes.'

PRAYER

****

Father today keep me steadfast on your word. When say we love you father make our actions speak for us. Father keep our ears open that we may hear from you. Keep our eyes open and alert to the things of you and only you. Father I thank you for your word and it is manifested in our lives. It will never return to you void in Jesus' name.

****

AFFIRMATION

BE WILLING TO
LET IT ALL GO
TO REGAIN
YOUR BALANCE

Most Daphinately

Daphne Hampton

DAY #56

PROVERBS 16:3

NEW INTERNATIONAL VERSION

³ Commit to the LORD whatever you do,
and he will establish your plans.

PRAYER

****

**Father God in the name of Jesus keep me humble, steadfast,
unmovable, unshakable, and upright before you. Lord every
vision you have placed in my heart shall come to pass.
Father continue to line me up to your word. Remove
anything that is not like you or contrary to your word in
Jesus' name.**

****

AFFIRMATION

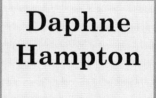

DAY # 57

PROVERBS 18:21

NEW INTERNATIONAL VERSION

²¹ The tongue has the power of life and death,
and those who love it will eat its fruit.

PRAYER

****

Father I just thank you for LIFE this morning. I thank you for yet another chance to get it right. To impact someone's life for the building of the kingdom. Father today I speak increase in all areas of our spiritual lives. Every person that read this prayer Father increase their FAITH on today father. Father you are worthy of all our praises today and forever more. Father finish a good work you started in each of us today in Jesus name.

AFFIRMATION

Daphne
Hampton

DO IT RIGHT
THE FIRST TIME!

Most Daphinatly

L.E.A.R.N.   L.O.V.E.   L.E.A.D

DAY #58

PROVERBS 20:11

NEW INTERNATIONAL VERSION

[11] Even small children are known by their actions,
so is their conduct really pure and upright?

PRAYER

****

Today I want to remind you that you have P.O.W.E.R. and it
lies inside you.

Father today stir up every GIFT you placed on the inside of
each of us from the creation of time.   Learn keep us
dedicated to this walk and the journey you have for me.

AFFIRMATION

319

DAY #59

PROVERBS 25:28

NEW INTERNATIONAL VERSION

²⁸ Like a city whose walls are broken through
is a person who lacks self-control.

PRAYER

****

**Father allow my Life to demonstrate love in all I do in your
son Jesus name. Continue to touch the hearts of each lady
connected to this project. Lord stir up every gift on the
inside of them. Continue to open doors in every area of their
lives. In Jesus name amen.**

AFFIRMATION

Queen Angela

I will become a better
LEADer by listening
More and talking less

SPEAK OVER YOURSELF

OVER THE NEXT
14 DAYS

14 resonates with expression of personal freedom. The numerology number 14 is a number of expressing personal freedom, including independence and self-determination.

Good Morning Affirmations

1. Today is a REALLY GOOD Day
2. Today I CHOOSE to BE HAPPY
3. Today I'm going to be my BEST SELF
4. Today I WILL be KIND to EVERYONE
5. Today I WILL be ONE with the UNIVERSE
6. Today I WILL make GOOD CHOICES
7. Today I WILL BELIEVE in MYSELF
8. Today I WILL BELIEVE in MIRACLES
9. Today I WILL be THANKFUL for what I HAVE
10. Today I WILL Be BRAVE, BOLD, and BEAUTIFUL
11. Today I WILL LOVE MYSELF and OTHERS
12. Today I AM POWERFUL
13. Today POSSIBILITIES are ENDLESS
14. Today IS GOING to be a GREAT DAY!

DAY # 60

PROVERBS 27:1

NEW INTERNATIONAL VERSION

27 Do not boast about tomorrow,

for you do not know what a day may bring.

PRAYER

****

Father allow the TRUTH to flow from me, allow your light to shine thru me . I shall not be moved

In Jesus name amen......

AFFIRMATION

Queen Angela
TODAY IS A
REALLY GOOD
DAY

DAY #61

ISAIAH 54:17

NEW INTERNATIONAL VERSION

[17] no weapon forged against you will prevail,
and you will refute every tongue that accuses you.
This is the heritage of the servants of the LORD,
and this is their vindication from me,"
declares the LORD.

PRAYER

****

P.O.W.E.R lies inside of you, Father stir up those gifts on the inside of us that we will walk in all that you ordained for us from the creation of time.

****

AFFIRMATION

Queen Angela
TODAY I
CHOOSE TO
BE HAPPY

DAY #62

PROVERBS 26:11-12

NEW INTERNATIONAL VERSION

[11] As a dog returns to its vomit,
so fools repeat their folly.
[12] Do you see a person wise in their own eyes?
There is more hope for a fool than for them.

PRAYER

■■

Father thru your word I'm able to discover what you have purposed me to do in this world. You have given us the power to receive understanding of your word.

****

AFFIRMATION

Queen Angela

TODAY I AM
GOING TO BE
MY BEST SELF

DAY # 63

2 PETER 2:22

NEW INTERNATIONAL VERSION

[22] Of them the proverbs are true: "A dog returns to its vomit,"[a] and, "A sow that is washed returns to her wallowing in the mud."

PRAYER

****

Father no matter what come at me today keep me stayed on you. Your will not mines In Jesus name amen …..

****

AFFIRMATION

Queen Angela

TODAY I WILL
BE KIND TO
EVERYONE

PHILIPPIANS 3:13

NEW INTERNATIONAL VERSION

[13] Brothers and sisters, I do not consider myself yet to have taken hold of it. But one thing I do: Forgetting what is behind and straining toward what is ahead,

PRAYER

****

Lord thank you for the word on today and reminding me that my past doesn't define me. Thanks for being my source and my supply line. Thank you for elevation and promotion.

.............PRESS......PRESS......PRESS......PRESS.........
....
▪▪▪

AFFIRMATION

Queen Angela
TODAY I WILL
BE ONE WITH
THE UNIVERSE

DAY #65

REVELATION 3:19

NEW INTERNATIONAL VERSION

[19] Those whom I love I rebuke and discipline. So be earnest and repent.

PRAYER

****

Father God keep me humble. Father today I ask if there is anything not like you to remove it right now. Line me up with your word, will and way. Never allow me to think I have POWER. I am powerless without you. Guide my oh Lord. In Jesus Name. amen

****

AFFIRMATION

Queen Angela
TODAY I WILL
MAKE GOOD
CHOICES

DAY # 66

PROVERBS 12:15

NEW INTERNATIONAL VERSION

[15] The way of fools seems right to them,
but the wise listen to advice.

PRAYER

****

Father God in the name of Jesus please keep me humble and
understand that the only POWER I have is in you. I am
POWERLESS. Lord teach me how to be the best version of
myself I can be every day In Jesus name.

****

AFFIRMATION

Queen Angela

TODAY I WILL

BELIEVE IN

MYSELF

L.E.A.R.N.   L.O.V.E.   L.E.A.D

DAY #67

PROVERBS 18:15

NEW INTERNATIONAL VERSION

¹⁵ The heart of the discerning acquires knowledge,
for the ears of the wise seek it out.

PRAYER

****

**Father keep me steadfast in your word. This is the day that
the Lord has made. I shall rejoice and be glad in the day!
Lord thank you for keeping us in the now this day.
Whatever shall be shall be and I thank you.**

****

AFFIRMATION

Queen Angela

TODAY I WILL

BELIEVE IN

MIRACLES

DAY #68

LUKE 2:40

NEW INTERNATIONAL VERSION

[40] And the child grew and became strong; he was filled with wisdom, and the grace of God was on him.

PRAYER

****

Father I thank you for favor right not. Keep me steadfast on your word allow your light to shine so bright thru us! In Jesus name.

****

AFFIRMATION

Queen Angela

TODAY I WILL BE THANKFUL FOR WHAT I HAVE

330

L.E.A.R.N.   L.O.V.E.   L.E.A.D

DAY # 69

1 PETER 2:2-3

NEW INTERNATIONAL VERSION

[2] Like newborn babies, crave pure spiritual milk, so that by it you
may grow up in your salvation, [3] now that you have tasted that
the Lord is good

PRAYER

****

Father keep me on task never wavering , give me the wisdom to
endure , thanks for extending your grace and mercy in Jesus
name.

****

AFFIRMATION

Queen Angela
TODAY I WILL BE
BRAVE
BOLD &
BEAUITFUL

DAY #70

PROVERBS 3:1

NEW INTERNATIONAL VERSION

Wisdom Bestows Well-Being

3 My son, do not forget my teaching,
but keep my commands in your heart,

PRAYER

****

Father I thank you on today for not giving up on me even when I
gave up on me. Father keep me focused on the things of you.
Keep me intentional about you, never let go in Jesus' name.

****

AFFIRMATION

Queen Angela
TODAY I WILL
LOVE
MYSELF & OTHERS

DAY #71

PROVERBS 4:5

NEW INTERNATIONAL VERSION

⁵ Get wisdom, get understanding;
do not forget my words or turn away from them.

PRAYER

■■

Father fill me with your truth, your word that it may lamp to my
dark path and I want stray in Jesus name.

✳✳

AFFIRMATION

 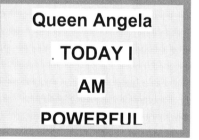

Queen Angela
. TODAY I
AM
POWERFUL

L.E.A.R.N.   L.O.V.E.   L.E.A.D

DAY # 72

PHILIPPIANS 4:9

NEW INTERNATIONAL VERSION

[9] Whatever you have learned or received or heard from me, or seen in me—put it into practice. And the God of peace will be with you.

PRAYER

****

Lord, I thank you for another day that wasn't promised me. Father I'm asking that you stir up the gifts that's on the inside of me to bring you glory and to help bring healing amongst your people. Father lead, guide and direct me to go out into the kingdom. Your will not mines. In Jesus name amen.

****

AFFIRMATION

Queen Angela

TODAY POSSIBILITES ARE ENDLESS

L.E.A.R.N.   L.O.V.E.   L.E.A.D

DAY #73

PSALM 32:8

NEW INTERNATIONAL VERSION

8 I will instruct you and teach you in the way you should go;
I will counsel you with my loving eye on you.

PRAYER

****

Father I thank you for breathing the breath of LIFE in me. Father
I thank you for extending your grace and mercy one more day
giving us the chance to impact the kingdom. Father allow me to
get a clear understanding of your word so I will not walk in error
or teach in error. Keep

me steadfast in your word.

AFFIRMATION

Queen Angela

TODAY

IS GOING TO

BE A GREAT DAY

335

DAY #74

1 THESSALONIANS 5:11

NEW INTERNATIONAL VERSION

[11] Therefore encourage one another and build each other up, just as in fact you are doing.

PRAYER

****

Father I thank you for reminding me that its not about me but about help my brothers and sisters to understand your truth. Lord continue to lead & guide us keep us on the plan you have for us remove that plan B and focus on that PLAN GOD HAS FOR YOU, don't know his plan for you? Seek him, study and show thou self-approve.

****

AFFIRMATION

Queen Angela

An excuse is worse and more terrible than a lie

DAY # 75

PROVERBS 1:7

NEW INTERNATIONAL VERSION

[7] The fear of the LORD is the beginning of knowledge,
but fools[a] despise wisdom and instruction.

PRAYER

****

Father continue to reveal your truth , light, wisdom and
knowledge. Father show me your way that I may be exactly who
you purposed me to be. No distractions shall come nah me.

AFFIRMATION

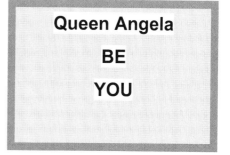

Queen Angela

BE

YOU

L.E.A.R.N.   L.O.V.E.   L.E.A.D

DAY #76

PSALM 25:4

NEW INTERNATIONAL VERSION

⁴ Show me your ways, LORD,
teach me your paths.

PRAYER

****

Father if you don't do it, it want be done. The word says "Only
fear the Lord, and serve him in truth with all your heart; for
consider how great things he hath done for you." Father lead and
direct us to do your will and not our will in Jesus name .
Amen…

AFFIRMATION

Queen Angela
STOP MAKING
ECXUSES

PSALM 25:5

NEW INTERNATIONAL VERSION

⁵ Guide me in your truth and teach me,
for you are God my Savior,
and my hope is in you all day long.

PRAYER

****

Father let your truth shine thru me and someone ask what must
they do to be saved. Guide and direct me oh Lord, all my HOPE
lies with you . In Jesus name AMEN.

AFFIRMATION
■■

Queen Angela

Legacy starts with
me...repeat after me I
HAVE THE POWER TO
CREATE A LEGACY

PROVERBS 12:1

NEW INTERNATIONAL VERSION

12 Whoever loves discipline loves knowledge,
but whoever hates correction is stupid

PRAYER

****

Father never allowing me to stop growing and seeking your truth.
Father every area of my LIFE where I lack please fill me with
your knowledge and understanding that I may help draw
someone unto you. Lord chastise me and keep me in your
WILL.

****

AFFIRMATION

Queen Angela
I am An
Influencer

L.E.A.R.N.   L.O.V.E.   L.E.A.D

DAY #79

DEUTERONOMY 8:5

NEW INTERNATIONAL VERSION

⁵ Know then in your heart that as a man disciplines his son, so
the LORD your God disciplines you.

PRAYER

****

Father thank you for correcting me and showing me when
I'm in error. Lord, I thank you for saving a wrench like me.

■■

AFFIRMATION

Queen Angela

I am A

Kingdom
Builder

341

DAY # 80

ACTS 20:20

NEW INTERNATIONAL VERSION

20 You know that I have not hesitated to preach anything that would be helpful to you but have taught you publicly and from house to house.

PRAYER

****

Father allow me to be bold with your word and to speak your truth with confidence and assurance. Allow me to help other to know you. Do not allow me to waver or shift. Keep me stayed on you! In Jesus name.

■■■

AFFIRMATION

Milagros Romero

I am grateful that in the word of God, I have found strength, peace, joy, good health, guidance, and great love.

DAY #81

LUKE 2:40

NEW INTERNATIONAL VERSION

[40] And the child grew and became strong; he was filled with wisdom, and the grace of God was on him.

PRAYER

****

***

Father continue to break and mold me into the daughter you have purposed me to be. Lord, please give me true wisdom and understanding of your word to apply it to my life for the building of the kingdom in Jesus name.

AFFIRMATION

Milagros-Romero

And as I seek to live my life according to God's plan for my life, I hold on to scriptures the assist in the renewal of my mind to achieve all that God designed for me.

L.E.A.R.N.   L.O.V.E.   L.E.A.D

DAY #82

PROVERBS 4:2

NEW INTERNATIONAL VERSION

² I give you sound learning,
so do not forsake my teaching

.

PRAYER

****
****

Father open my inner ear that I will hear and comprehend your
word and your truth .

In Jesus name.

****

AFFIRMATION

QUEEN ANGELA
BROKEN TO BE
MENDED & MOLDED
BY THE CREATOR

DAY # 83

PROVERBS 9:9

NEW INTERNATIONAL VERSION

⁹ Instruct the wise and they will be wiser still;
teach the righteous and they will add to their learning.

PRAYER

****
**

Father I thank you for being exactly who you are in Jesus' name.
Today I'm grateful and thankful for LIFE, health and strength.
Father teach me oh Lord, fill me with your wisdom and allow me
to learn continually.

AFFIRMATION

QUEEN ANGELA

I

AM

CONTENT

DAY #84

TITUS 2:1

NEW INTERNATIONAL VERSION

2 You, however, must teach what is appropriate to sound
doctrine.

PRAYER

****

Thank you, Lord, for allowing me the ability to teach and lead
your people in LOVE. Father keep me on the straight and
narrow only speaking and sharing your truth. In Jesus name.

****

AFFIRMATION

QUEEN ANGELA
LIFE DOSEN'T
HAVE TO BE
PERFECT IN ORDER
TO BE AMAZING

PROVERBS 22:6

NEW INTERNATIONAL VERSION

⁶ Start children off on the way they should go,
and even when they are old they will not turn from it.

PRAYER

****

Father thank you for my parents and each person you ordained to
be a part of my life. The good the bad and the ugly YET I
STAND your word will never return to you void. Keep me
humble and steadfast I will not be moved.
■■■

AFFIRMATION

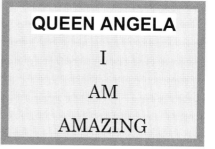

QUEEN ANGELA
I
AM
AMAZING

DAY # 86

ROMANS 15:4

NEW INTERNATIONAL VERSION

⁴ For everything that was written in the past was written to teach us, so that through the endurance taught in the Scriptures and the encouragement they provide we might have hope.

PRAYER

****

Father thank you for instructions for us to live by while we inhabit this temple and earth. Father I thank you for not giving up on me and leaving me in the darkness. I am thankful today for the very LIFE you have given me to bring you glory. In Jesus name AMEN.

AFFIRMATION

■■

QUEEN ANGELA
WHEN IT RAINS LOOK FOR RAINBOWS

348

DAY #87

PROVERBS 10:7

NEW INTERNATIONAL VERSION

[7] The name of the righteous is used in blessings,[a]
but the name of the wicked will rot.

PRAYER

****

Father thank you for allowing me another chance to impact lives
and to speak your truth to draw others to the kingdom. Lord
keep me Holy and under your wings. Cover me going and
coming. Father order my steps. In Jesus name Amen.

****

AFFIRMATION

QUEEN ANGELA
SEE THE
GOOD
IN YOURSELF

DAY #88

PSALM 32:8

NEW INTERNATIONAL VERSION

[8] I will instruct you and teach you in the way you should go;

I will counsel you with my loving eye on you

PRAYER

****

Father thanks for allowing me the opportunity to impact the world for the building of the KINGDOM. In Jesus name.

****

AFFIRMATION

QUEEN ANGELA

I

Am

Determined

L.E.A.R.N.   L.O.V.E.   L.E.A.D

DAY # 89

JAMES 1:5

NEW INTERNATIONAL VERSION

[5] If any of you lacks wisdom, you should ask God, who gives generously to all without finding fault, and it will be given to you.

PRAYER

****

Father continue to fill me with your word of truth, that I may continue to share your goodness across this world. In Jesus name amen.

****

AFFIRMATION

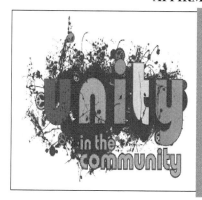

QUEEN ANGELA

He closed that door

too open 1 more!!!!

351

L.E.A.R.N.   L.O.V.E.   L.E.A.D

DAY #90

JOHN 14:26

NEW INTERNATIONAL VERSION

[26] But the Advocate, the Holy Spirit, whom the Father will send in my name, will teach you all things and will remind you of everything I have said to you

PRAYER

****

Father today I say YES. Yes, to your will and Yes to your Way. Guide, lead and direct my every step. Fill me Lord that others will see you thru me. In Jesus name.

AFFIRMATION

QUEEN ANGELA

FAITH

LOVE

FAMILY

352

DAY #91

MATTHEW 28:19-20

NEW INTERNATIONAL VERSION

[19] Therefore go and make disciples of all nations, baptizing them in the name of the Father and of the Son and of the Holy Spirit, [20] and teaching them to obey everything I have commanded you. And surely I am with you always, to the very end of the age."

PRAYER

****

Lord thank you for going before us and setting order and revealing your truth. Lord thank you for being just who you said you would be in your word. Thank you, LORD.

****

AFFIRMATION

QUEEN ANGELA

GOOD THINGS SHALL HAPPEN. DON'T WAIT MAKE IT HAPPEN

353

DAY # 92

PSALM 25:4

NEW INTERNATIONAL VERSION

⁴ Show me your ways, LORD,
teach me your paths.

PRAYER

****

Father teach me your ways and I want stray. I may fall but I know with your word and knowledge I will never stay down. Thank you father for bringing me out of the darkness. You didn't have to but you did and I'm forever grateful.

AFFIRMATION

QUEEN ANGELA
ALWAYS STAY
HUMBLE
&
KIND

1 CORINTHIANS 13:4-5

NEW INTERNATIONAL VERSION

⁴ Love is patient, love is kind. It does not envy, it does not boast, it is not proud. ⁵ It does not dishonor others, it is not self-seeking, it is not easily angered, it keeps no record of wrongs.

PRAYER

****

Lord teach me how to love genuinely, true and honestly. Instill in me patient (to endure) and kindness (how to be). Father never let me be envious, boast or be proudful. Keep me humble and steadfast on your word. Slow to angry but quick to show LOVE. Less of me and more of you Lord. In Jesus name AMEN.

****

AFFIRMATION

QUEEN ANGELA

WANT TO KNOW WHO YOU ARE?

FIND OUT WHO THE CREATOR IS.

L.E.A.R.N.   L.O.V.E.   L.E.A.D

DAY #94

1 CORINTHIANS 13:6-8

NEW INTERNATIONAL VERSION

[6] Love does not delight in evil but rejoices with the truth. [7] It always protects, always trusts, always hopes, always perseveres.

[8] Love never fails. But where there are prophecies, they will cease; where there are tongues, they will be stilled; where there is knowledge, it will pass away.

PRAYER

****

Father continue to equip me with spirit of Love and all things needed to help lead your people. Remove me in flesh out of the way and allow your spirit man to speak thru me. Father thank you in Jesus name.

****

AFFIRMATION

QUEEN ANGELA

R.E.N.E.W.

RELEASE   EVALUATE

NAVIGATE

ELABORATE   WISDOM

L.E.A.R.N.   L.O.V.E.   L.E.A.D

DAY # 95

1 JOHN 4:7-9

NEW INTERNATIONAL VERSION

7 Dear friends, let us love one another, for love comes from God.
Everyone who loves has been born of God and knows
God. 8 Whoever does not love does not know God, because God
is love. 9 This is how God showed his love among us: He sent
his one and only Son into the world that we might live through
him.

PRAYER

****

Father this day I am reminded that LOVE is key. Love comes
from God and if you lack love you lack God . Father fill me with
your spirit of love that I will never lack and pour out into your
people for the building of the kingdom.

****

AFFIRMATION

| QUEEN ANGELA |
| R.E.S.E.T. |
| RELEASE   ENGERIZE SEPARATE |
| EPHASIS   TAKE ACTION |

DAY #96

ROMANS 5:8

NEW INTERNATIONAL VERSION

[8] But God demonstrates his own love for us in this: While we were still sinners, Christ died for us.

PRAYER

****

Thank you for grace and mercy, you keep blessing us.

THANK YOU JESUS YOU ARE WORTHY AND YET FAITHFUL. In Jesus name.

AFFIRMATION

QUEEN
ANGELA
BEGIN
EACH DAY
WITH A
GRATEFUL
HEART

DAY #97

1 JOHN 3:18

NEW INTERNATIONAL VERSION

[18] Dear children, let us not love with words or speech but with actions and in truth.

PRAYER

****

Father thanks for reminding me that you are in control and that I am powerless. I am only able to obtain POWER thru you and your will for my life. Continue to break and mold me into the son/daughter you have purpose me to be even before the creation of time. Father I thank you today. In Jesus name amen

****

AFFIRMATION

QUEEN ANGELA

THE BEST IS YET TO COME

PROVERBS 10:12

NEW INTERNATIONAL VERSION

[12] Hatred stirs up conflict,
but love covers over all wrongs.

PRAYER

****

Father I thank for yet another day that was not promised me. Father today I
ask if there is anything we lack or stand in need of father open the door
right now in Jesus name. Father stir up those things in that will bring you
glory and honor your name. Your will father not mines. Use me Lord for
your GLORY!!

****

AFFIRMATION

QUEEN ANGELA

HE MADE ME
IN HIS IMAGE

DAY #99

1 Corinthians 16:14

New International Version

[14] Do everything in love.

PRAYER

****

I PRAISE YOU TODAY BECAUSE YOU DIDN'T HAVE TO. Father today show me how to LOVE more. Father has I yield to you, fill me with your spirit that it may shine so bright, and someone will see you thru me and say HOW can I be SAVED.

****

AFFIRMATION

QUEEN ANGELA
I
AM
THE CHOSEN

DAY #100

1 PETER 4:8

NEW INTERNATIONAL VERSION

[8] Above all, love each other deeply, because love covers over a multitude of sins.

PRAYER

Since I was a little girl this scripture has always reminded me that love draws and love covers. Lord I thank you for showing me what true love was over these last 100 days, I have been tested, tried and thru it all but I WILL NOT BE MOVED. I want shake, bend or break because daily I'm learning and understanding more of you . Father I thank you for bringing me into the LIGHT.

****

AFFIRMATION

QUEEN ANGELA
STUDY AND
SHOW THYSELF
APPROVED

DAY # 101

ROMANS 12:9-10

NEW INTERNATIONAL VERSION

[9] Love must be sincere. Hate what is evil; cling to what is good. [10] Be devoted to one another in love. Honor one another above yourselves.

PRAYER

****

Father I thank you for truly giving me a heart for your people . I thank you for this journey even when I didn't understand. I thank you for brining me out of the darkness to be an impact to the world for building of Kingdom. Father keep me humble and steadfast on your word.

****

AFFIRMATION

QUEEN ANGELA

C.R.E.A.T.E

YOUR OWN WAY!!!

DAY #102

ROMANS 13:10

NEW INTERNATIONAL VERSION

[10] Love does no harm to a neighbor. Therefore love is the fulfillment of the law

PRAYER

****

Father your will not mines. Father I thank you because you didn't have to but you woke me up this morning and started me on my day. Lord I thank for setting order in my LIFE and allowing me to discover the you inside of me. Thank you, lord, for opening my eyes and ears.

AFFIRMATION

QUEEN ANGELA G.U.I.D.E. MY WAY OH LORD!

DAY #103

MARK 12:31

NEW INTERNATIONAL VERSION

31 The second is this: 'Love your neighbor as yourself.'[a] There is no commandment greater than these.

PRAYER

****

Father your will not mines. Father remove me out of the way today. Lord teach me how to look pass the flesh and see the GOD inside others, Father teach me all your ways and remove me out of the way.

AFFIRMATION

QUEEN
ANGELA
RENEW
MY
MINDSET

1 PETER 5:6-7

NEW INTERNATIONAL VERSION

[6] Humble yourselves, therefore, under God's mighty hand, that he may lift you up in due time. [7] Cast all your anxiety on him because he cares for you.

PRAYER

****

Father today I just want to say thank you. Father you didn't have to but you did. Your grace & your mercy you extended one more day. Father if you don't do another thing, I am grateful for all that you have done. You are worthy of all our praises.

****

AFFIRMATION

QUEEN
ANGELA
I WILL
NOT BE
MOVED

DAY #105

PROVERBS 3:3-4

NEW INTERNATIONAL VERSION

[3] Let love and faithfulness never leave you;
bind them around your neck,
write them on the tablet of your heart.
[4] Then you will win favor and a good name
in the sight of God and man.

PRAYER

****

Father lead us in your truth today allow your love for us to shine

thru our actions. Guide our actions today, allow your word to be

LIFE to this journey today. Allow someone to see you in Jesus'

name.

AFFIRMATION

QUEEN
ANGELA

I

AM

UNSTOPPABLE

DAY #106

Luke 6:31

New International Version

[31] Do to others as you would have them do to you.

PRAYER

****

Father today I am reminded that I was born into sin yet with natural sight but yet still blind. Father I thank you for bringing me out of the darkness into the marvelous light.

AFFIRMATION

QUEEN ANGELA WHEN I DIE IN THE FLESH HE WILL WAKE UP MY SPIRIT

DAY # 107

PROVERBS 3:3-4

NEW INTERNATIONAL VERSION

³ Let love and faithfulness never leave you;
bind them around your neck,
write them on the tablet of your heart.
⁴ Then you will win favor and a good name
in the sight of God and man

PRAYER

****

Father I thank you for saving and setting me free. You opened
my eyes and ears to the ways of you and how I can gain eternal
LIFE . Father I thank you for your son Jesus on today. Thanks
for sending him to be an example for us in the flesh. Father
continue to perfect the spirit man in me for your glory.

AFFIRMATION

QUEEN
ANGELA
HE IS
MY
LIGHT

L.E.A.R.N.   L.O.V.E.   L.E.A.D

DAY #108

PSALM 86:15

NEW INTERNATIONAL VERSION

15 But you, Lord, are a compassionate and gracious God, slow to anger, abounding in love and faithfulness.

PRAYER

****

Father keep me humble and steadfast on your word. Allow me to an example of LOVE. Fill me up with your spirit. Lord your will not my will. In Jesus name. I shall not be moved.

AFFIRMATION

QUEEN
ANGELA

I AM

A

SAVANTE

DAY #109

1 JOHN 4:12

NEW INTERNATIONAL VERSION

[12] No one has ever seen God; but if we love one another, God lives in us and his love is made complete in us

PRAYER

****

AGAPE love unconditional love. Father I thank you for this journey of finding true love, your love.

L- looking pass the flesh in seeing the Jesus in me

O- Overcoming and defeating all obstacles that come our way thru Jesus.

V- understanding your value, your worth and knowing no one can put a value on you.

E- evolving to the next level in Christ not willing to stay where you are .

Father today I thank you for revealing your word to me so that I may continue to be lamp unto the world.

AFFIRMATION

QUEEN ANGELA I AM EXTRAORDINAR

DAY # 110

JOHN 13:34

NEW INTERNATIONAL VERSION

[34] "A new command I give you: Love one another. As I have loved you, so you must love one another.

PRAYER

****

Father today allow my LIFE to be a LAMP to someone, that they will see you thru me and not me in the flesh. Less of me Lord and more of you. Allow me to IMPACT lives for the kingdom today in Jesus' name. Your will not mines.

AFFIRMATION

QUEEN
ANGELA
I MAY FALL
BUT I WANT
STAY DOWN

L.E.A.R.N.   L.O.V.E.   L.E.A.D

DAY #111

LEVITICUS 19:18

NEW INTERNATIONAL VERSION

18 "'Do not seek revenge or bear a grudge against anyone among your people but love your neighbor as yourself. I am the LORD.

PRAYER

****

Father God you are in control, I'm reminded of your grace & mercy you extend every day. Giving us another chance to get it right. Today I choose to walk in LOVE. Continue to line me up with your word. In Jesus name amen.

AFFIRMATION

QUEEN
ANGELA
I
SHALL
SOAR

DAY #112

PROVERBS 17:17

NEW INTERNATIONAL VERSION

[17] A friend loves at all times,
and a brother is born for a time of adversity.

PRAYER

****

Father teach me how to be a true friend .

Show me how to truly love.

Keep me humble and true to your word.

AFFIRMATION

QUEEN
ANGELA
REACH FOR
THE
GOD IN
YOU

DAY # 113

MATTHEW 22:37

NEW INTERNATIONAL VERSION

[37] Jesus replied: "'Love the Lord your God with all your heart and with all your soul and with all your mind.'

PRAYER

****

Father thanks for reminding me that LOVE covers & draws. Father thank you for showing us how to LOVE thru your word. Father keep me steadfast & unmovable, allow me to be a doer of the word. Guard my heart, mind body and soul. Line me up with your word and will for my life. Your way father not mines. In Jesus name AMEN.

****

AFFIRMATION

QUEEN
ANGELA
I AM A
BLESSING

375

DAY #114

ROMANS 13:8

NEW INTERNATIONAL VERSION

⁸ Let no debt remain outstanding, except the continuing debt to love one another, for whoever loves others has fulfilled the law.

PRAYER

****

Father thanks for reminding me that we owe no one anything but to LOVE them. Father thank you for allow me another chance to get it right and to IMPACT someone else LIFE. Father allow someone to see you in me and not me in the flesh never let it be about me.

AFFIRMATION

QUEEN
ANGELA
.GOD
IS MY
PORTION

DAY #115

PSALM 143:8

NEW INTERNATIONAL VERSION

8 Let the morning bring me word of your unfailing love,
for I have put my trust in you.
Show me the way I should go,
for to you I entrust my life.

PRAYER

****

Father fill me with a fresh oil, that your light shall shine all so
bright and somebody shall be saved on today.

NEVER LET YOUR LIGHT BURN OUT IN ME.

IN JESUS NAME.

AFFIRMATION

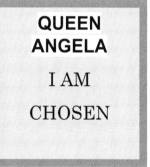

QUEEN
ANGELA

I AM

CHOSEN

GALATIANS 5:13

NEW INTERNATIONAL VERSION

[13] You, my brothers and sisters, were called to be free. But do not use your freedom to indulge the flesh[a]; rather, serve one another humbly in love.

PRAYER

Father, I'll trust you when I can't see you. I'll trust you when I can't trace you. I'll trust you because you are my belief system and I have been made to trust you. Father you cared enough for me to bring me out of the darkness. Father you cared just enough to allow us to share your goodness with someone else. SO today father I thank you again for all that you have done, is doing and shall do. You are not slack in your giving and I thank you in Jesus name.

AFFIRMATION

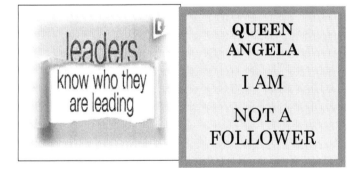

QUEEN
ANGELA

I AM

NOT A
FOLLOWER

DAY #117

1 THESSALONIANS 3:12

NEW INTERNATIONAL VERSION

[12] May the Lord make your love increase and overflow for each other and for everyone else, just as ours does for you

PRAYER

****

Father shower us with your LOVE on today. Allow your light to shine so bright thru us on today. May somebody see YOU in me today and ask how can I be saved. Lord please never allow your light in me to burn out keep me filled with your oil.

AFFIRMATION

QUEEN ANGELA

I AM FILLED WITH HIS P.O.W.E.R

DAY #118

1 JOHN 4:19

NEW INTERNATIONAL VERSION

¹⁹ We love because he first loved us.

PRAYER

****

Father, I thank you for free will but I also thank you for wisdom on how to serve the kingdom humbly without being in the flesh. Father please keep me steadfast unmovable in your word. No weapon , no tongue, no demon, nothing like you shall come NAH me. In Jesus name , your will for my LIFE your will and not mines AMEN.

****

AFFIRMATION

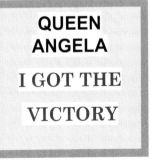

QUEEN ANGELA

I GOT THE VICTORY

DAY # 119

1 CORINTHIANS 13:13

NEW INTERNATIONAL VERSION

[13] And now these three remain: faith, hope and love. But the greatest of these is love.

PRAYER

****

Father I reminded that your word "faith without works is dead" I know that your word will not return to you void so as I wait for your word to manifest in my LIFE I pray that you will renew my strength to endure, stand and not be moved. This is my prayer. In JESUS name I pray.

****

AFFIRMATION

QUEEN ANGELA

HE SHALL SUPPLY ALL MY NEEDS

JOHN 15:13

NEW INTERNATIONAL VERSION

¹³ Greater love has no one than this: to lay down one's life for one's friends.

PRAYER

****

Father, continue to open my eyes and ears so that I will hear from you and be led by your spirit. We may never understand all the wonders of you father. Don't allow me to get to consumed with cares of this flesh but to stay focused and keep my mind stayed on you and the P.O.W.E.R within me.

****

AFFIRMATION

QUEEN ANGELA
I AM A NEW
CREATURE IN
CHRIST

DAY #121

PSALM 5:8

NEW INTERNATIONAL VERSION

⁸ Lead me, LORD, in your righteousness
because of my enemies—
make your way straight before me.

PRAYER

****

Father, I thank you for choosing me for this journey. I thank you
for every person connected to this project. I speak overflow in
every area of their lives. Favor shall find them. Father you watch
over this project and movement, allow it to be ALL ABOUT
YOU, Father keep me humble and steadfast on your word.
Continue to a great work in me. Watch over your word until it is
performed in our lives according to your will for each of us!!

AFFIRMATION

QUEEN ANGELA
I AM
I AM

CLOSING

PRAYER

✳ ✳ ✳ ✳ ✳ ✳ ✳ ✳ ✳

Father I thank you for this opportunity to pour into to lives in hopes that we can Educate, Empower, and Encourage someone to come out of their current DARK state of being. Father I pray over every person that took the time to share thru this devotional. Father now we give it back to you to do what you would have it to do in the lives of your people here on this earth.

Father I pray that this book will not just sit on a shelf but will be your daily source of strength to those that may be weak in their walk with you. Father may something from these pages speak to their heart on this day and the days to follow. In Jesus name amen amen.

In Jesus name It is so

AFFIRMATION

Bringing H.E.A.L.ing, in the city in H.E.E.L.S.

L3 MOVEMENT (LEARN, LOVE & LEAD)

RESOURCES AND BUSINESSES to equip you thru,

LEARNing
LOVing
LEADing

(3alac2016@gmail.com)

facebook.com/aspire2inspiremagazine

SADIOR RADIO

CATCH ME LIVE EVERY SUNDAY
8AM-10AM (book your sot today)
DOWNLOAD THE "sadior radio" APP
FROM GOOGLE OR APPLE PLAY

D.A.M.O.N. looks

Determined And Motivated Online
Network a part of O.N.E dynasty ....
Every Sunday Night 6pm(EST) I invite
YOU TO BE A guest on my platform for a
face to face interview. Giving our
5+ million listeners/followers a chance to
see us LIVE via video, 32 spots available
book your spot today

Commissioner Angela Thomas Smith
1. Host of walk in purpose W/ Angela
2. Host of D.A.M.O.N. speaks
3. Host of D.A.M.O.N. looks

UP CLOSE & PERSONAL W/ ANGELA
ON BEHALF OF ASPIRING AUTHORS
MAGAZINE

INTERVIEWS ARE CONDUCTED EVERY
MONDAY 12PM & 1PM EST ONLY 2021 ONLY
104 INTERVIEWS WILLBE CONDUCTED IN
2021 RESERVE YOUR SPOT TODAY.........

WALKING
IN
PURPOSE

with Angela

D.A.M.O.N. network walk in
purpose with Angela
Walk in purpose with Angela airs Live from Lagos
Nigeria every 4 weeks on wednesday. My desire is to
highlight guest that are walking in their purpose. My
desire is to share Love & Hope to Educate , Empower
& Encourage someone to walk in purpose. BOOK
YOUR SPOT TODAY (ONLY 24 GUEST IN 2021)

I Am H.E.R. International
Release H.E.R. sounds News...

YOU CAN CATCH ME LIVE EVERY SATURDAY 10AM-12PM EST LIVE RIGHT HERE
ON FACEBOOK VIA STREAMYARD. I am 1 of 4 host on this amazing Broadcast...

MONDAY MOTIVATION

EVERY MONDAY MORNING FROM 9AM-9:30AM I WILL BE LIVE WITH
MY CO-HOST ON BLOGTALKRADIO CALL INTO 515-602-9744 PRESS 1
TO CHAT WITH US.........
PLEASE GO FOLLOW ME AND SHARE MY LINK........
blogtalkradio.com/mondaymotivationhourofpower

L.E.A.R.N.   L.O.V.E.   L.E.A.D

CONNECT WITH THE VISIONARY
QUEEN OF COLLABORATIONS
ANGELA THOMAS SMITH

https://linktr.ee/QueenofCollaborations

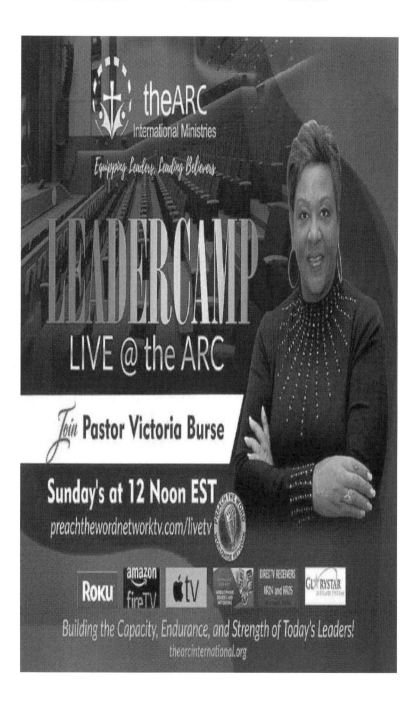

L.E.A.R.N.   L.O.V.E.   L.E.A.D

TRIED
TESTED
TRIUMPHED
EVERY MONDAY
6 PM EST LIVE
ON LINKEDIN
TO BE MY GUEST
DIRECT MESSAGE ME
(SMALL FEE REQUIRED)

PSALM 121 LIFTED US IN 2020

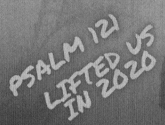

HOSTED
BY THE ORIGINAL
"QUEEN OF COLLABORATIONS"
ANGELA THOMAS SMITH

Tonight 9:30PM EDT
www.blogtalkradio.com
type in search
NgoziTime also dial
in @ 516-453-9133
& press 1 to join the
conversation brought
to you by Looking Glass
Entertainment

WE ARE ON NIGHTLY, HOWEVER MY
SHOW AIRS EVERY 4 WEEKS ON
WEDNESDAY

L.E.A.R.N.   L.O.V.E.   L.E.A.D

LEARN
LOVE
LEADL.E.A.R.N. ◇L.O.V.E.◇L.E.A.D = L3 MOVEMENT WE
ARE THE CHANGE WE DESIRE TO SEE IN OUR
COMMUNITIES.....
Sh'Aunta Moore, FOREWORD
Cheneria Osbourne, Pamela J Hayes, & Angela Thomas Smith
CO-AUTHORS (3 WOMEN OF FAITH)
****
contributing Authors

1. Shana Gourdine,
2. Leesa Michelle,
3. Charlotte Simon,
4. Mary Kennedy,
5. Rolanda T Pyle,
6. Author Michelle Cain,
7. Kenya Reid,
8. Tiffany S Hooks,
9. Tamara Singleton,
10. Constance Mckinsey Neal,
11. Nakia Bradley,
12. Samantha J Jackson,
13. Aquintas Jones,
14. Blaque Diamond,
15. Allie West,
16. Shelia c Lewis,
17. Diana Hill,
18. Shelly Knox,
19. Keywana Wright-Jones,
20. Mama Forbes,
21. Sheela Wiley,
22. Leah Legrone,
23. Stephanie Johnson-Rice,
24. Carrie L Thomas,
25. J Senay Spurgeon

397

26. Tajika Giles,
27. Voncille Morton,
28. Karen Stanton Kennedy,
29. Glendora Dvine,
30. Mattie Daniels,
31. Janice Mayes,
32. Kim C Rice,
33. Laura Worthy Crawford,
34. Betty J Lewis,
35. Temekia Glenn,
36. Ollie Thompson,
37. Qualisha K Benson,
38. Destiny Stanford,
39. Sharon Randolph,
40. Tina Michelle Baker,
41. Deborah Ivey,
42. Nia Murdock,
43. Camaria Cocoa Fenton,
44. Angela Cole Claiborne,
45. Jessica Starks,
46. Daphne Hampton,
47. Chioma Chinaka Chigozie-Okwum,
48. Kadian Palmer Asemota,
49. Malik Beckett,
50. Tonya Vernon,
51. Victoria Burse,
52. .Tabitha Stevens,
53. Valerie Young,
54. Lisa Hayes,
55. Barbara Brown Stewart,
56. Terrie Sylvester,
57. Dr LaDonna Hollis,
58. Tamela Lucus,
59. Cheryl LeGrand,
60. Donna Garey,
61. Tasha Downing.

62. Renita Singleton,
63. Tiara Synder,
64. Barbara Palmer
65. Cheryl Jones
66. Dr Kimberly Thomas,
67. Marcia Harton,
68. Shylia Nix,
69. Kimberly Moore,
70. Jane Hamick,
71. Dominique E. Jones,
72. Bridget N Tharpe
73. Alexandria J Garrett,
74. Lashone L Grimes,
75. Shante Reed,
76. Queashar L Halliburton,
77. Kela Calvin,
78. Kashinda T Marche,
79. LaMia Pierce,
80. Miranda Starks,
81. Shannon Starr,
82. Vernae Taylor,
83. Chavonne D Stewart,
84. Chantal Jennings,
85. Annette Martin,
86. Chyrel J Jackson ,
87. Lyris D Wallace,
88. Tia Melvin,
89. Teresa S McCurry,
90. Lakia Bennett,
91. Telecia Stanton,
92. Savannah "Savy" Dawson,
93. Tando Tullia Keke,
94. Arica P Quinn,
95. JoAnne F Blake,
96. Susan Turner.

97.   JonQuil Medley,
98.   Clare Ezeakacha,
99.   Annette Worwell,
100. Tammy Myers,
101. Delicia Mayes ,
102. Antionette Osborn,
103. Kim Knight,
104. Pauline Atkinson,
105. Eleanor R Tye,
106. Nichole Henderson,
107. Chinyelu Uduchuckwu-Akpaka,
108. Char Prince,
109. R.C Nicole,
110. Jazzmin Raine,
111. Marvette Deadwyler,
112. Essie Davis,
113. Chinchila Jonesia,
114. Deborah A Franklin,
115. Sheena Gee,
116. Nicho Charisse,
117. Lisa Renee Halliburton,
118. Margaret Parker,
119. Monica Reese,
120. Ashley Abraham,
121. Mechell Davis,
122. LaTonya Mullins,
123. Chaka Davis Smith,
124. Zipporah Israel,
125. Myra Starks,
126. Pamela Edwards,
127. Dr.Karen D Lomax,
128. Beverly White,
129. Sandra Gamble,
130. Auset Atun Re,
131. Andree M Harris,
132. Myra Williams Armstead,
133. Milagros Romero
134. Julie Thomas

YOU CAN FOLLOW MOST
OF US ON FACEBOOK &
INSTAGRAM......
TO FOLLOW THE
L3MOVEMENT
https://www.facebook.com/L3moveme
nt

THANKS FOR SUPPORTING AND
FOLLOWING THE MOVEMENT
WE ARE THE CHANGE FOR THE
NEXT GENERATION.

PLEASE SHARE AND KEEP
Learning, Loving and Leading the
way.
I love you and aint 1 thing you can do
about it!!!!   *Queen Angela Tomas Smith*

DELAYED BUT THE GOD I SERVE NEVER
FAILS. DON'T LET DISTRACTIONS KEEP
YOU FROM DOING WHAT GOD HAS
CALLED YOU TO; THEY WILL COME
THAT'S THEIR JOB BUT THEY WILL
NEVER WIN. GOD WILL ALWAYS PREVAIL
IF YOU STAND ON HIS WORD. PSALM 121
LOOK TO THE HILLS (BE REMINDED GOD
IS IN CONTROL DON'T FAINT OR GET
WEART IN WELL DOING)

I PRAY THIS BOOK DOES EXACTLY WHAT
GOD DESIRE IT TO DO FOR YOU .

I THANK GOD FOR EACH PERSON THAT
SOWS INTO THIS SERVICE MINISTRY I AM
CALLED TO LET MY BROHERS AND
SISTERS KNOW THEY HAVE PURPOSE IN
THIS EARTH REALM AND THAT GOD
DIDN'T DROP THEM OUT THE SKY HE
PLACED THEM HERE WITH PURPOSE.
NOT SURE WHAT YOUR PURPOSE IS LET'S
CONNECT

3alac2016@gmail.com

Linktree

https://linktr.ee/QueenofCollaborations

Made in the USA
Middletown, DE
08 March 2023

26381258R00223